HISTORY OF TIMOR-LESTE

Frédéric B. Durand

Cover photographs and credits (from top left)

1　Timorese people in Marobo | Brigitte Clamagirand
2　Timorese dancers in Marobo | Brigitte Clamagirand
3　Arrival of Louis-Claude de Freycinet and the French expedition in Dili, 1818
4　Timorese king Dom Boaventura de Manufahi
5　Timorese with spears | Brigitte Clamagirand
6　Governor Celestino da Silva
7　Traditional house in Los Palos
8　Timorese women weaving in the 1920s
9　José Ramos Horta during a demonstration in 1975
10　Pope John Paul II in Dili, October 1989 | Reproduced by permission of Servizio fotografico de l'O.R.
11　The East Timorese flag is raised in front of the United Nations headquarters in New York on September 27, 2002, in the presence of Xanana Gusmão, Kofi Annan, and José Manuel Durão Barroso | UN Photo/ Mark Garten
12　Nicolau Lobato and Francisco Xavier do Amaral, 1975 | Stéphane Dovert
13　Xanana Gusmão signing the new Timor-Leste Constitution, May 20, 2002, | Images Max Stahl

ISBN: 978-616-215-124-8

Translated from the original French edition, *42 000 ans d'histoire de Timor-Est*, by Frédéric B. Durand (Toulouse: Editions Arkuiris, 2009). Translation by Geoffrey C. Gunn.

An attempt was made to cite the sources of all illustrations. For claims involving any unattributed illustrations, please contact the publisher.

Maps by Frédéric B. Durand

First published in English in 2016 by
Silkworm Books
430/58 Soi Ratchaphruek, M. 7, T. Mae Hia, A. Mueang Chiang Mai, Thailand 50100
info@silkwormbooks.com
www.silkwormbooks.com

Typeset in FreightNeo Pro 10.5 pt. by Silk Type

Printed and bound in the United States by Lightning Source

Foreword

Dr. Frédéric Durand, the author of *42.000 anos da história de Timor-Leste*, is preeminent among historians specializing in Timor-Leste and holds an authentic passion for all things Timorese. The French edition of his book was published in 2010, and now this new English translation will reach an even wider readership.

History of Timor-Leste is a stimulating book. It reminds us that Timor-Leste was not just born in 2002, the year that the United Nations recognized its independence, or even in 1975, on the day of the unilateral declaration of independence by the Fretilin party. In reality, the history of Timor-Leste goes back to at least 1515, with the arrival of the first Portuguese ships in demand of sandalwood. According to Professor Durand, the history of Timor-Leste spans a period of forty-two thousand years. We must therefore thank the author for his unflagging commitment to studying and accurately presenting the country's early history and prehistory. Professor Durand's many publications cover the entire ancient, modern, and contemporary history of Timor-Leste.

In addition to his dedicated and persistent research on Timor-Leste history, Professor Durand is unique in his pedagogical approach: his books contain original excerpts and images by which he aims to teach the Timorese people in general, and the children and young people in particular, to know and study their own history in order to preserve the memory of their ancestors and transmit this cultural and historical knowledge to future generations.

Noteworthy features of Professor Durand's publications about Timor-Leste are the brief and concise descriptions of events and the abundant presentation of photographs, most of which are even unknown to the Timorese, showing significant people, places, artifacts, fauna, and flora. His works also include a generous archive of ancient maps and illustrations. All this draws readers into the history of Timor and invites them to experience and relive past events.

On behalf of the Timorese people, I wish to express my great appreciation and admiration to Professor Frédéric Durand for this important contribution to our historical record.

Mgr. Carlos Filipe Ximenes Belo
Nobel Peace Prize laureate
Porto, Portugal
August 2016

Contents

Louis Klaco, son of the king of Dili, 1818.

Dona Joana, wife of the captain-major of Dili, 1818.

Antonio, young man from the Failacor kingdom of Timor, 1818.

Introduction

Writing a concise history requires making some hard choices. I have decided to write simply and straightforwardly, avoiding detailed citations as much as possible. For the sake of clarity, I have chosen to use a chronological approach. Contrary to what many people tend to believe, there is a history and even a prehistory of East Timor that began long before the arrival of the Portuguese. Archaeological findings date back at least forty-two thousand years.

This book, which has been published in French and in a bilingual Tetum-Portuguese edition, was conceived as a practical tool to contribute to the knowledge and dissemination of East Timorese national history from a Timorese vantage point. Although many books and articles have been written on the history of Timor, they are generally not very well known or not easily accessible, especially to the East Timorese. Yet, in the context of the national construction of the Democratic Republic of Timor-Leste, it is essential that the Timorese people reclaim their history, because it is from the knowledge of their ancestors, and from traditions, legends, and events of the past that they will be able to shape the present and the future.

Although this book is primarily intended for use by teachers and educators, it will also be useful to those who wish to acquire a broad overview of the country's history.

The volume has been divided into five parts and fifteen chapters. The most commonly accepted forms of names and historical figures have been used. In order to facilitate the reading, it was decided to limit the number of references and to avoid footnotes. The sources are grouped at the end in three sections: a list of major books on the global history of Timor, a bibliography of works on the island, and a list of articles and books that served as the main sources for each chapter.

Several essential books that cover the long history of East Timor deserve special mention: the history of East Timor in four volumes by the Portuguese

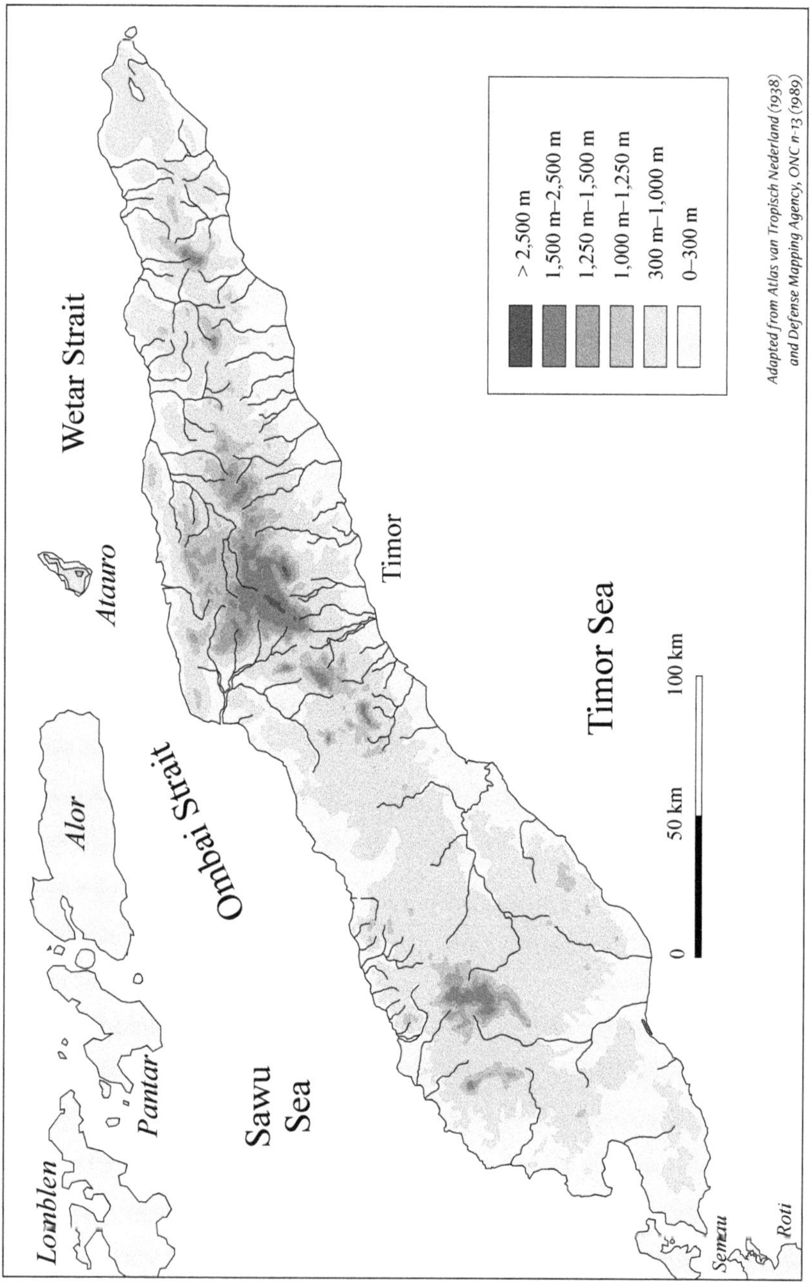

Legend:

- > 2,500 m
- 1,500 m–2,500 m
- 1,250 m–1,500 m
- 1,000 m–1,250 m
- 300 m–1,000 m
- 0–300 m

Adapted from Atlas van Tropisch Nederland (1938)
and Defense Mapping Agency, ONC n-13 (1989)

Wetar Strait

Atauro

Timor

Alor

Ombai Strait

Timor Sea

Lomblen

Pantar

Sawu
Sea

Semau

Roti

0   50 km   100 km

Map 1: Topography of Timor

historian Luna de Oliveira in 1949 (reissued in 2004), books in French by Gabriel Defert (1992) and by René Pélissier (1996), those in English by James Dunn (1983) and Geoffrey C. Gunn (1999), and a more recent book in Portuguese by Barbedo de Magalhães (2007).[1]

I have outlined some aspects of East Timorese history in a geo-historical atlas published in 2002 (translated into English in 2006 and Portuguese in 2010) and in two other books on the history of Christianity (2004) and on travels to Timor (2006).[2]

We do hope that this work will encourage East Timorese researchers to deepen their knowledge and to build their own national history.

Mythical Times

Researching the memory of societies involves many specializations including archaeology, history, linguistics, but also anthropology and even genetics. We must remember that history is a "construction" in which the researcher decides to emphasize or focus on one aspect or another. Thus history can take the form of royal chronicles, economic and social history of dominant populations, or the history of minorities.

But memory is not only historical. It is also partly mythical. Numerous myths exist in East Timor. They may differ depending on the ethno-linguistic group. Nevertheless, the three main myths deserve to be recalled:

1. Timor was born of the body of an old, stranded, fossilized crocodile. This crocodile offered a ride to a young boy who had saved his life in the past, allowing him to establish a country. Indeed, seen from space or arriving by

---

1. Luna de Oliveira, *Timor na História de Portugal* (Lisbon: Fundação Oriente, 2004); Gabriel Defert, *Timor-Est, le génocide oublié* (Paris: L'Harmattan, 1992); René Pélissier, *Timor en guerre, le crocodile et les Portugais (1847–1913)* (Orgeval: Pélissier éditeur, 1996); James Dunn, *Timor: A People Betrayed* (Milton, Queensland: Jacaranda Press, 1983); Geoffrey C. Gunn, *Timor Loro Sae: 500 Years* (Macau: Livros do Oriente, 1999); António Pinto Barbedo de Magalhães, ed., *Timor-Leste: Interesses internacionais e actor locais* (Porto: Afrontamento, 2007).

2. Frédéric B. Durand, *East Timor: A Country at the Crossroads of Asia and the Pacific* (Chiang Mai: Silkworm, 2006); *Catholicisme et protestantisme dans l'île de Timor 1556–2003* (Bangkok: IRASEC, 2004); and *Timor 1250–2005, 750 ans de cartographie et de voyages* (Bangkok: IRASEC, 2006).

Jacques Arago, 1822. Private collection

Crocodile hunting in Timor

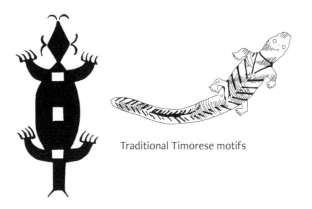

Traditional Timorese motifs

boat, the shape of the island conjures up the silhouette of a saurian. This shape can be found in many East Timorese decorative patterns.

Geology should also take account of this image, which gives Timor a unique origin among the surrounding islands. Indeed, the island of Timor is not volcanic, though many of its neighbors are. It was formed by the thrust of the Australian tectonic plate sinking gradually under the Asian plate. Travelers also attested to the presence of many crocodiles in the island up to the twentieth century.

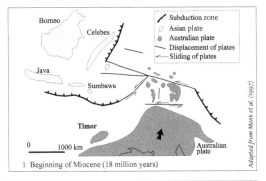

1. Beginning of Miocene (18 million years)

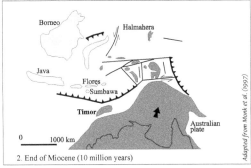

2. End of Miocene (10 million years)

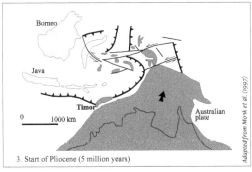

3. Start of Pliocene (5 million years)

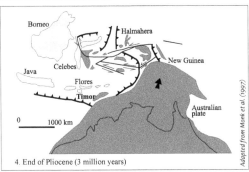

4. End of Pliocene (3 million years)

Map 2: Geological evolution of Timor

2. Many Timorese groups maintain that they had an external origin, and that they came to the island in boats. Archaeology and linguistic research tends to confirm that the population of Timor was a result of successive waves of migration over more than forty thousand years.

3. Some ethno-linguistic groups on the island consider that their region is the center of the world where humankind emerged. Others think that a rope or liana was attached to the sky, forming a conduit for ancestors or spirits, some of which still remain in the island. These beliefs illustrate the deep attachment of many East Timorese to the spiritual realm. Indeed, one might wonder whether there was a spiritual component to the tremendous power that finally freed the country after so many years of occupation by as formidable a force as Indonesia.

These myths incline us to modesty in our process of historical "reconstruction." They invite us to remember that spirituality is an important component of societies, particularly in the Asia-Pacific region. A history must not be a list of facts and events. It must also strive to understand the particular culture and traditions so as not to betray the soul of the people.

Construction of a traditional house in Marobo, in the center of the island of Timor

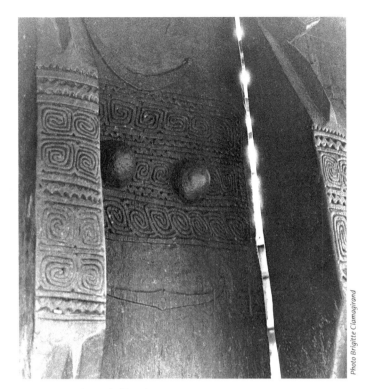

Photo Brigitte Clamagirand

Entrance to a house in Marobo

Photo Stéphane Dovert

Photo Brigitte Clamagirand

Statues of ancestors

Young Timorese girls in the 1960s.

Part I

ANCIENT TIMES

Ceremony in Marobo in the 1960s

Photo Brigitte Clamagirand

Chapter 1

PREHISTORIC TIMOR

Overview

Leaving aside mythical stories, the first vestiges of human habitation in Timor date back at least 42,000 years. They are probably related to the first Melanesian migration waves linked to present autochthonous populations of New Guinea and Australia.

About 4,500 years ago, new migrations occurred, undoubtedly by Austronesian people originating from mainland Asia and traveling through the island of Taiwan. They brought new crops and techniques with them.

Timor appears to have been little affected by the civilizations of the Bronze Age at the turn of the Christian era. Instead, it was climate change between 1100 and 1600 that might have led to cultural transformations, including the construction of fortifications on the hills, known as *tranqueiras*.

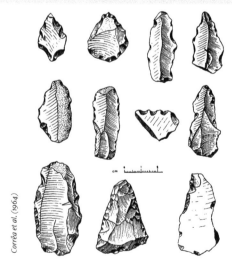

Corrêa et al. (1964)

Silex tools found in East Timor

1.1 A first phase of Melanesian or Papuan settlement

The discovery of stone tools and cave paintings by early Portuguese archaeological explorations prove that Timor was inhabited for a very long time, even though the techniques at the time did not allow precise dating. In the late 2000s, human artifacts were found by archaeologist Sue O'Connor that date back about 42,000 years. Stone tools and drilled shells probably used as decoration were discovered in the cave of Jerimalai, at the eastern tip of the island. Remains of meals were also discovered, along with sea turtles, ocean fish, bats, and giant rats. Many other cave sites help us reconstruct some aspects of Timorese prehistory.

People may have come to Timor as early as 50,000 or 60,000 years ago, when *Homo sapiens* first crossed the Southeast Asian archipelago from Asia to Australia. Over the ages, cross-marriage and migration have no doubt partially mixed genetic lines and the languages spoken. However, it is still possible to connect the Melanesian languages of Timor (Bunaq, Fataluku, Makasi, Makalero, Maku'a) to the Berau region in western New Guinea. With the exception of Bunaq, these linguistic groups are mainly located in the eastern half of Timor island.

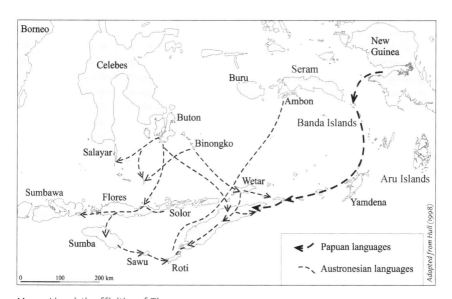

Map 3: Linguistic affinities of Timor

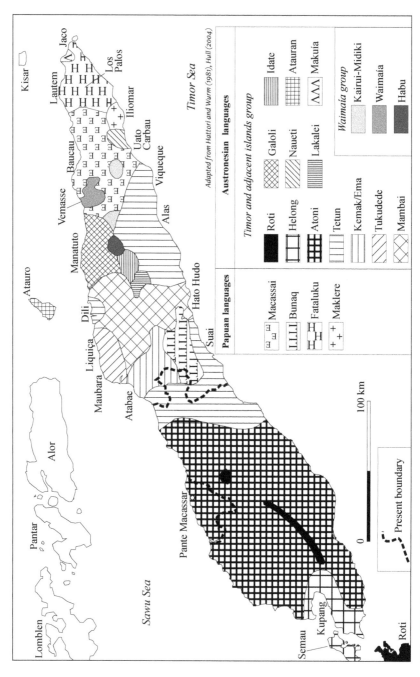

Map 4: Main languages of Timor

The lifestyle and economy of these people was certainly based on hunting, gathering, fishing, and farming, although it is impossible, for the moment, to trace the evolution and possible changes over the millennia. Among the crops that were likely collected or planted were the sago palm (*Metroxylon sagu*, valued for the starch found in the pithy center of its stems), tubers such as taro (*Colocasia esculenta*), nuts, palm sugar (*Arenga pinnata*), and perhaps Job's tears (*Coix Laccryma-jobi*). The latter cereal is attested in Timor at least 17,400 years ago, but so far there is no proof that it was either grown or harvested.

Migration led to the introduction of animals such as the cuscus, a type of possum probably introduced from New Guinea, and some rodents. Fishing was also an important activity. Shellfish hooks estimated to be 10,500 years old and the remains of large fish show that the Timorese had complex fishing technology and that they ventured to the high seas. Vestiges of earth ovens also show that people had sophisticated culinary practices.

Between 30,000 and 12,000 years ago, profound changes occurred due to rising sea levels caused by melting ice at the end of the last ice age. The waters rose by about 120 meters to reach the current level. The ancient coastal sites were gradually submerged, forcing people to settle in higher areas. Pigments found in caves, dating back more than 29,000 years, suggest that these Melanesian people might have practiced rock art. Most designs however seem to be related to a second great wave of migration.

A. Mesnel after Temmink, in Wallace (1872, 5-235). Private collection

Colijn (1911)

Man harvesting sago from a palm tree

The cuscus of Timor (*Phalanger orientalis*)

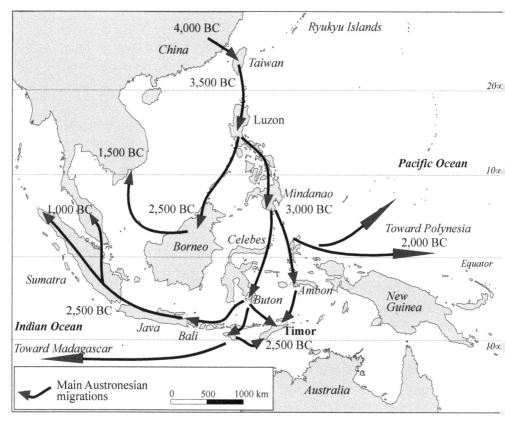

Map 5: Austronesian migrations from northern Asia

O'Connor (2003; 118)

Boats depicted in rock art in Lene Cece cave

Hunters depicted in rock art in Illi Kérékéré and Suntarléu

1.2 The Austronesian contribution

The history of Southeast Asia was marked by a series of migrations of people called Austronesian or Malayo-Polynesian. Those people, probably originating from mainland Asia via the island of Taiwan, sailed to the southern islands 5,500 years ago. They passed through the Philippine archipelago, Borneo, Celebes, and the Moluccas. The diffusion of "Malaysian" (Malayo-Polonesian) languages through the islands of Southeast Asia (Malay, Indonesian, Tagalog), including many Timorese languages (Tetum, Mambai, Kemak) and the languages of Polynesia and Madagascar, are linked to these migrations.

In Timor, the linguistic affinities suggest that there were two main paths of propagation, the first via Buton, southeast of Sulawesi (formerly Celebes), and the second via Ambon in the Moluccas. Those people would have arrived on boats from five to fifteen meters long and propelled by paddles, oars, and perhaps square sails, as can be conjectured from cave paintings. These paintings illustrate the major themes of rock art around the world: hands in negative view, geometric shapes, human and animal silhouettes. Men are sometimes drawn with weapons for fighting or for hunting.

The Austronesians brought with them the art of pottery and many animals, including dogs, pigs, goats, and cattle. The Austronesians are also possibly responsible for the dissemination of rice, but it has not been possible to date its introduction. Although the grain played a very minor role in Timorese agriculture before the nineteenth century, the arrival of these people undoubtedly changed and enriched the local cultures

Photo Frédéric Durand

Illi Kérékéré cave and rock art

Photos Álvaro Eugenio Neves de Fontoura

Portraits of Timorese people in the 1930s

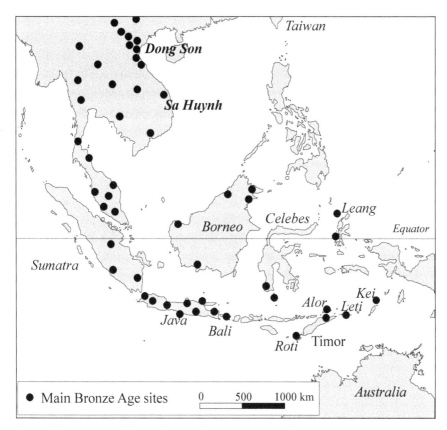

Map 6: Main archeological sites from the Bronze Age in Southeast Asia

1.3 Changes over the past two millennia

At the turn of the Christian era, Southeast Asia experienced a new wave of influence with the rise of cultures that excelled in bronze metallurgy. The two best known cultures are Dong Son in present-day northern Vietnam, which manufactured the famous bronze drums, and Sa Huynh culture in central Vietnam. Austronesian populations were probably at the origin of the later.

Many drums or bronze objects from this period have been found in mainland Southeast Asia and in the archipelago, such as in the Sunda Islands—Java, Bali, Flores, Roti, Leti, Alor—along with the Moluccas. The larger drums are up to 1.85 meters high. This culture does not seem to have had a strong influence on Timor. Only one ancient bronze ring was discovered in East Timor in the 1960s by archaeologist Ian Glover dating from between twenty-three hundred and two thousand years ago.

Another change that probably did have a significant impact in Timor was the intensification of the El Niño effect, which disrupts the monsoon and brings prolonged drought in Asia. Studies of marine and lake sediments show that El Niño was stronger and more frequent between 1100 AD and 1600 AD. Archaeologist Peter Lape hypothesized that climate changes could have led to food shortages and famine in Timor, as well as increased conflicts between groups. Give or take a few decades, this period is concomitant with the development of fortified settlements known as *tranqueiras*. They were mainly established in Timor between 1150 and 1650, with a peak phase of construction between 1450 and 1650.

These fortified sites, many of which still remain in East Timor, were built on hilltops to take advantage of the topography. Their limestone walls can measure from 1.5 to 4 meters in height, and 1 to 3 meters at their base. They could extend over an area of 500 to 3,000 square meters.

The arrival of Chinese ships in the thirteenth century, followed by Muslim traders and the Portuguese, might have brought about the construction of these defensive structures.

Photo Frédéric Durand

Remains of a *tranqueira*, early twenty-first century

Timorese warriors

Revista Missões (1950)

Chapter 2

MAJOR EXTERNAL CONTACTS
BEFORE THE PORTUGUESE

Overview

The island of Timor had been regularly visited by Chinese ships from the mid-thirteenth century onwards especially in search of sandalwood.

Traders from the Middle East and from Java also participated in this trade prior to the arrival of the Portuguese. By that time trading activities were mainly concentrated on the coast of western Timor.

Chinese junk, early twentieth century

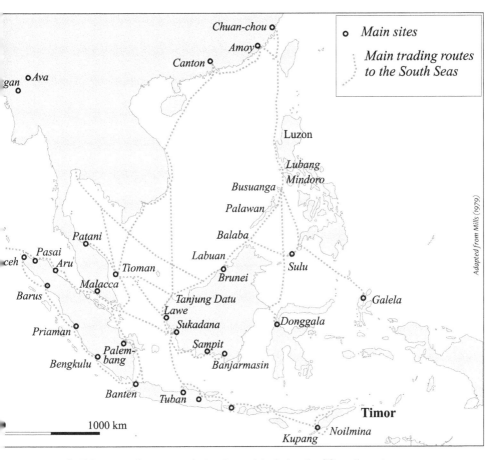

Main sites

**Main trading routes
to the South Seas**

Chuan-chou
Amoy
Canton
gan ○Ava

Luzon

Lubang
Busuanga Mindoro
Palawan

Patani
Pasai
ceh Aru
Barus
Tioman
Malacca
Priaman
Palem-
Bengkulu bang
Banten Tuban

Balaba
Labuan
Brunei
Tanjung Datu
Lawe
Sukadana
Sampit
Banjarmasin

Sulu

Galela

Donggala

Timor
Noilmina
Kupang

1000 km

Adapted from Mills (1979)

Map 7: Main Chinese maritime routes in Southeast Asia during the fifteenth century

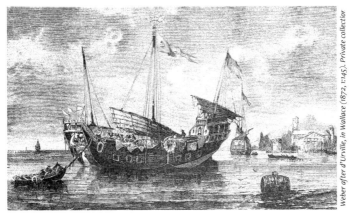

Weber after d'Urville, in Wallace (1872, 1:145). Private collection

Chinese junk, nineteenth century

2.1 Timor in Chinese trading networks in the thirteenth century

The existence of vast forests of sandalwood (*Santalum album*) attracted many seafarers and primarily the Chinese. Sandalwood was used to manufacture incense and fragrant wood objects. The growth of trade between China and Timor might be due to the depletion, by the twelfth century, of resources of precious wood in India and in Pegu, now Myanmar.

Several Chinese texts mention Timor, the oldest being the *Chu-Fan-Chï* (Records of Foreign Peoples) dated about 1250 AD and, a century later, the *Tao-I-Chih-Luëh* (Brief Accounts of the Island Nations). They offer descriptions of life in the island:

> The mountains have no trees other than sandalwood, in great abundance. Such things as silver and iron bowls, Western (Indian) silk cloth, and colored kerchiefs are traded.
>
> There are chiefs in twelve places altogether. The fields are suitable for grain. The climate is not even; the days are hot and the nights are cold.
>
> Men and women cut their hair short and wear cotton shirts of black cloth. In the marketplace, the price of wine and meat is cheap.
>
> Those arriving there catch diseases, and many died. If they are to avoid this, they must remain within the confines of their ships. If one is exposed to the wind and rain, one contracts disease and develops a high temperature. It leads to inevitable death.

These Chinese texts confirm the existence of regular trading activities in a dozen localities. The manuscript also shows the fear of disease by Chinese travelers in Southeast Asian islands. Profit expectations, however, justified maintaining the trade. Thus, Timor is mentioned in several guidebooks for Chinese seafarers throughout the fifteenth century.

Another Chinese text, the *Shun Fêng Hsiang Sung* (Fair winds for escort), dated around 1430, provides navigation information for hundreds of routes to the South Seas. Fourteen localities in Timor are explicitly mentioned. This confirms the existence of a significant trade centered on sandalwood, even

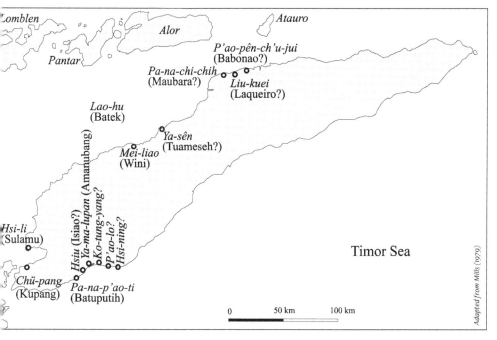

Map 8: Main Chinese trading posts in Timor during the fifteenth century

Chinese objects found in Timor

before the arrival of Europeans. The text also shows that the Chinese were mainly in contact with kingdoms in the western and northern part of the island.

2.2 Timor in Muslim trading routes

The Timorese were not cut off from the rest of Southeast Asia. They also had relations with peoples from neighboring islands, including Wetar and Kisar, which long held vassalage links with local groups in Manatuto and Vemasse. Meanwhile, the island of Timor was visited by vessels from Java and the Persian Gulf. The Javanese poem *Nagara Kertagama* speaks of "Timur" as a dependency of the kingdom of Majapahit, but with no details, and there is no evidence that this territory was the island of Timor. Moreover, research on Majapahit shows that the extent of its political control has often been exaggerated. Majapahit actually controlled only East Java and Madura. Javanese sailed to Timor, but like the Chinese, it was in order to trade with other kingdoms.

Manuscripts by Arab pilots Ahmad ibn Majid in 1462 and Sulaiman al-Mahri in 1511 (the year the Portuguese seized Malacca) synthesize the understandings of Muslim seafarers of that time. From their descriptions of navigation and orientation, it has been possible to draw a map revealing their knowledge. Sites mentioned on the Malay Peninsula and Sumatra are many, but the islands beyond Java were scarcely known.

It is also worth noting that, for them, "Timor," which means east in many Austronesian languages, did not correspond to a specific island. At that time, the name Timor referred to all of the islands southeast of Java. In 1511, the islands brought together under the name of Timor were divided into two sub-groups: Lor Timor (northern Timor) and Kidul Timor (southern Timor), each group consisting of four or five islands that are difficult to identify today.

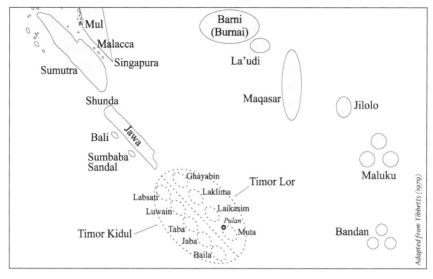

Map 9: Southeast Asia according to Arab seafarers around 1511

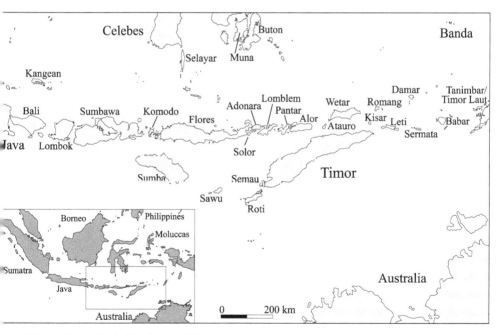

Map 10: Lesser Sunda Islands east of Java

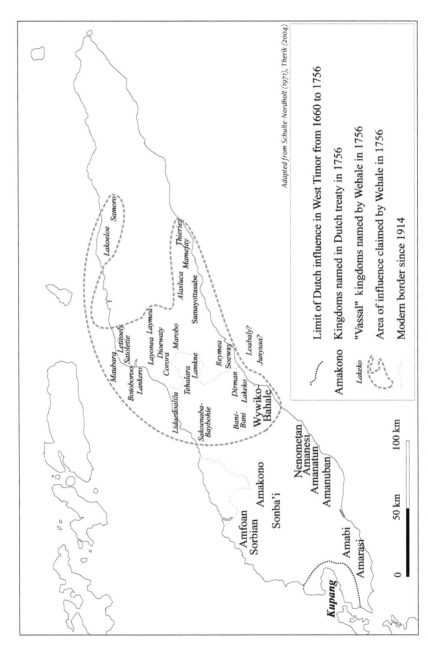

Map 11: Extent of the Waiwiku-Wehale "empire" in the eighteenth century

Adapted from Schulte-Nordholt (1971), Therik (2004)

Lakoeloe Samorri

Maubara Letitoely Satoletie
Botoboro Lankero
Layonea Laymea
Dioewaty
Corova Marobo
Tehalara
Lamkne
Lidgedoaililu

Alashica Thieriex
Mameflay
Samayottasabe

Reymea
Socway
Loabaly?
Junysaa?

Bani-Bani Dirman Lakeko
Sakoenaba-Baybohie Wywiko-Bahale

Amfoan
Sorbian Amakono
Sonba'i

Nenometan
Amanesi
Amanatun
Amanuban

Amabi
Amarasi

Kupang

Limit of Dutch influence in West Timor from 1660 to 1756

Amakono Kingdoms named in Dutch treaty in 1756

Lakeko "Vassal" kingdoms named by Wehale in 1756

Area of influence claimed by Wehale in 1756

Modern border since 1914

0   50 km   100 km

Chapter 3

TRADITIONAL SOCIETIES

Overview

Despite their diversity, Timorese cultures showed many common features, including an attachment to the sacred (*lulik*) in the organization of society. Some kingdoms recognized a higher authority, notably the Waiwiku-Wehale kingdom at the center of the island. But this was more of a spiritual authority than a political one.

Traditionally, the kings had limited powers and ruled within a system of government called an "aristocratic republic" by Portuguese observers.

Traditional societies also produced sophisticated forms of arts and crafts.

3.1 Common values among diverse cultures

It is important to emphasize the diversity of cultural traditions in East Timor. In a country whose size lies between that of Lebanon and Kuwait, there are now more than twenty ethno-linguistic groups that have evolved over the ages. Several elements of continuity can nevertheless be identified.

Most of the cultures were originally based on a dual conception of the world. Bipartition was the predominant principle, which identifies pairs of polar opposites, such as female/male, indoor/outdoor, stationary/active. However, the elements of these pairs were not mutually exclusive. On the contrary, society needed to find a balance between them in order to live in harmony.

Traditional societies attached great importance to the sacred. An equilibrium had to be maintained between the forces of the universe and the human world. Stones, trees, and water sources were often regarded as receptacles of spirits or supra-human forces. The world of the living was linked to the world of the dead. Numbers had a great significance in rituals. The concept of house (*uma*) was very strong and viewed as part of a pyramidal structure. Hamlets of four to ten houses (*aldeia*) were gathered into villages (*suku*). Groups of villages composed kingdoms. Every village had two sacred houses (*uma lulik*). This organizational structure continues today, even though Catholicism has spread widely over the country during the past decades.

Many ethno-linguistic groups were matrilineal, meaning that women played a key role in the society. The first Portuguese narratives attest that kingdoms were frequently headed by queens. Over the last centuries, the role of women has declined, notably due to foreign influence.

Photo Ruy Cinatti

Ricefields in Timor

Photo Ruy Cinatti

Timorese in front of a megalith, probably with religious significance. Many megaliths could still be seen until colonial times.

Photo Ruy Cinatti

Timorese woman wearing a tiara, a sign of her nobility

Ceremony in the Marobo area

Photo Brigitte Clamagirand

3.2 Alliances, power, and social organization

The traditional kingdoms of Timor were hierarchically structured into several levels: the king or *liurai*, the notables or noblemen (*datos*), the commoners or free men, and the so-called slaves. The king had limited powers. This fact led Portuguese observers to describe Timorese kingdoms as aristocratic republics, where the assembly of notables could remove a king.

The so-called slaves would better be called "dependents." In traditional systems, they were regarded as members of the family. They could buy their freedom and be freed. When this happened, they assumed the status of their former master. If the latter was a nobleman, the slave would also become a *dato*.

There have been hundreds of kingdoms in Timor. The relations between them were strongly influenced by their relative status. The kingdoms that "gave women" had a higher spiritual status, being donors, than those that "took women." The exchange of women was accompanied by a system of dowry (*barlaque*). The dowry could be very high, up to several dozen buffaloes.

In the sixteenth century, many kingdoms of central Timor recognized the spiritual authority of the kingdom of Waiwiku-Wehale, with which the kingdoms of Sonba'i and Camenasse were affiliated. These kingdoms sometimes fought ritual wars (*funu*) that included headhunting.

3.3 Culture and art, traditional technologies and material production

The societies of Timor did not build great monuments as did those of Cambodia, Vietnam, or Java, although some of their *tranqueiras* are impressive. However, Timorese people developed many notable skills and cultural practices. Traditional techniques in agriculture, hunting, fishing, and the medicinal use of plants, which have long been denigrated, are beginning to be recognized and acclaimed in anthropological works.

Timorese handicrafts, such as weaving, pottery, metalwork, and basketry, have produced objects that command a high value, notably woven cloth (*tais*), wood sculpture, and silver and gold jewelry. Timorese architecture is

Fishing at Bé Malai

Timorese woman decorating earthenware

Adapted from Cinatti (1987)

Maubisse/
Same/
Laclubar

Ataúro

Baucau/
Ossu

Bobonaro

Díli

Liquiça

Manatuto

Baucau

Lautém

Aileu

Viqueque

Bobonaro

Manufahi
Same

Ainaro

Lautem/
Los Palos

Oecussi
Ambeno

Cova-Lima

West Timor

Viqueque

Suai

0   50 km

Map 12: Different types of traditional houses

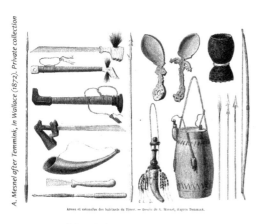

A. Mesnel after Temmink, in Wallace (1872). Private collection

Traditional Timorese weapons,
tools, and utensils

Photo Ruy Cinatti

Dance performance by young girls in the
Suai area

also very sophisticated, with many different styles of houses from region to region.

One of the richest traditions is probably that of singing and music. In the 1960s, the Australian musicologist Margaret King compared Timorese music to the works of Johann Sebastian Bach:

> The musical life of the Timorese possesses a richness and complexity of structure and design surpassed only by their fine textiles. For the person fortunate to penetrate beyond the apparent monotonous repetition, it provides a rare and rewarding experience.
>
> This inherent feeling of texture in their various art forms is a very striking factor among the Timorese, but to be fully appreciated it demands the absorbed and sympathetic attention of the observer. As with the complex polyphonies of Bach, deep concentration is rewarded by deeper satisfaction.

These comments from an anthropologist show the sophistication of Timorese art and culture—specifically music—in contrast to what many outsiders might tend to assume.

Photo Ruy Cinatti

Drum dance in the Suai area

Timorese men carrying sandalwood swords

Part 2

THE FIRST CONTACTS
WITH THE WEST

Private collection

Portuguese coin of East Timor

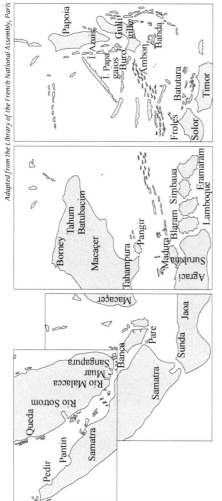

Map 13: Southeast Asia according to Portuguese cartographer Francisco Rodrigues, 1512

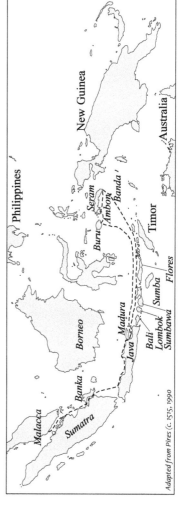

Adapted from Pires (c. 1515, 1990)

Map 14: The voyage of Francisco Rodrigues, 1512

Chapter 4

THE BEGINNING OF WESTERN INFLUENCE, 1512–1642

Overview

The first mention of Timor by the Portuguese is found on a map dated 1512. However, the Dominican priests, initially based on the island of Solor, only began regular sandalwood trade with Timor in the 1550s, especially with the kingdoms of western Timor.

The Dutch first arrived in Timor in 1613 but they did not establish a permanent settlement. The Portuguese influence increased from 1641, with the conversion of several kings and queens to Catholicism. In 1642, their victory over the renowned kingdom of Waiwiku-Wehale gave them further advantage.

4.1 Initial contact with the Portuguese, 1512–1613

After arriving in India in 1498 and conquering Malacca in 1511, the Portuguese launched an initial expedition to the Spice Islands in 1512. The cartographer Francisco Rodrigues drew a map of the region, on which Timor appears with the words, "the island of Timor, where the sandalwood originates." On January 6, 1514, Captain Rui de Brito Patalim wrote to King Manuel I from Malacca. He reported that Timor was an island beyond Java that produced a great amount of sandalwood, honey, and beeswax.

In his book *Suma Oriental*, completed in 1515, Tomé Pires confirms the information on trading networks in Asia:

> Between the islands of Sumbawa and Solor, there is a wide strait where the islands of sandalwood are. All these islands to the east of Java are called Timor, because in the language of the country *timor* means

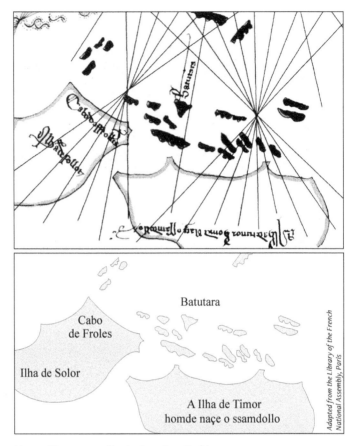

Map 15: Timor according to Francisco Rodrigues, 1512

east. The islands of Timor have pagan kings. There is plenty of white sandalwood. It is very cheap because there is no other wood in the forests.

Merchants bring white cloth and coarse cotton cloth from India, and in return for a few goods, they load their junks with sandalwood. The trip to Timor pays, but is not very safe.

The Portuguese probably began direct trade with Timor around 1515. At first, they were mainly in contact with kingdoms in the western and southern part of the island, namely Kupang, Lifau (Oecussi), and Camenasse. In January 1522, at the time of the Magellan-Elcano circumnavigation, the Italian António Pigafetta stayed for twenty days in Timor. He found traces of a Portuguese presence but did not meet any Portuguese himself.

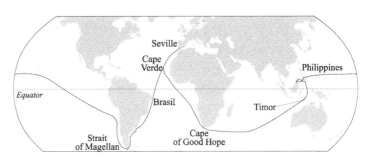

Portuguese stamp portraying
Ferdinand Magellan

Map 16: The first circumnavigation of the world by Magellan
and Elcano, 1519–1522

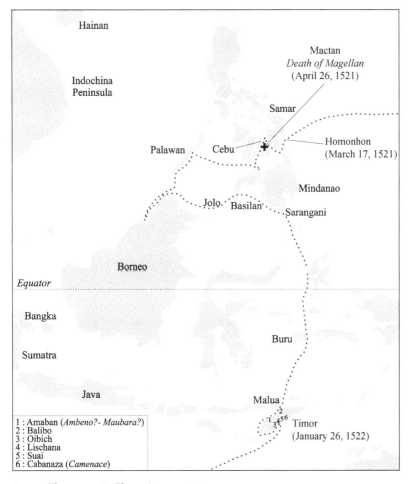

Map 17: The voyage to Timor, January 1522

The great Portuguese poet Luis Vas de Camões, author of *The Lusiads* (*Os Lusíadas*) recalling the voyages of explorer Vasco de Gama, lived in poverty in Asia from 1553 to 1567. He spoke of Timor in his epic poem:

> And there is also Timor,
> with its forests of sandalwood,
> salutary and scented.

Portuguese poet Luís Vas de Camões

A treatise on botany, written by Garcia da Orta in 1563 in Goa, confirms that the island of Timor had many ports, including four at which the Portuguese were trading regularly: Mena, Matome, Camenasse, and Servião. The Portuguese did not immediately settle in Timor. In the 1550s, their main base was the island of Solor, which was smaller and more convenient to stay on during the monsoon. Dominican priests were supervising sandalwood trade with the kings of Timor. In 1589, the first church was built in Mena east of Oecussi, but it was abandoned a few months later.

Nevertheless, the Portuguese had acquired knowledge of a significant portion of the island. In 1613, the Malaccan-based cartographer Manuel Godinho de Erédia drew a detailed map of Timor. It shows five important kingdoms, four in the north around present-day Oecussi: Servião, Siciale,

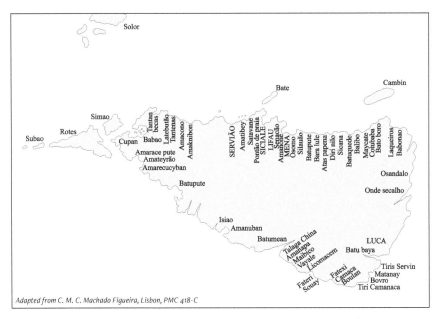

Adapted from C. M. C. Machado Figueira, Lisbon, PMC 418-C

Map 18: Timor according to Portuguese cartographer Manuel Godinho de Erédia, 1613

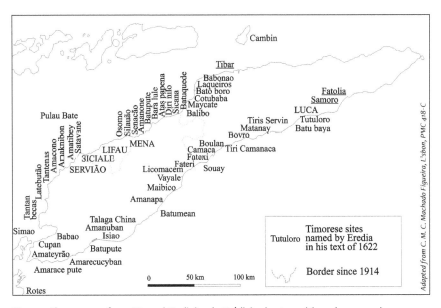

Map 19: Place names from Manuel Godinho de Erédia's chart, positioned on a modern map

Lifau, and Mena; and one on the south coast: Luca. In all, Erédia distinguished more than fifty sites in mainland Timor, not including the adjacent islands of Atauro and Batek, and the islands off Kupang.

4.2 The beginning of rivalry between the Portuguese and the Dutch, 1613–1642

In April 1613, the year Erédia drew his maps, the Dutch East Indian Company (VOC) arrived in Timor for the first time. While Captain Apollonius Schot was blockading the port of Solor, he sent two boats to Timor. Like the Portuguese, the Dutch were primarily interested in the sandalwood trade. The rulers of Kupang and Amanuban, who wanted to get rid of the Portuguese presence, proposed that the Dutch sign a treaty of alliance and build a fort on their land at the western end of the island.

On April 20, 1613, when the Portuguese finally capitulated in Solor, the Dutch took a census. There were 1,000 people, including 250 blacks and mestizos able to bear arms, 30 Portuguese, and 7 Dominican friars. On Timor itself, there were 89 white and 450 mixed-race people. The Portuguese were allowed to return to Malacca, but the VOC did not take advantage of this move and refrained from establishing a permanent settlement in Timor. They merely left a representative on the island of Flores. This negligence allowed the Portuguese to return to Solor and Timor the following years. In 1629, the

Sixteenth-century Portuguese coin (*left*) and seventeenth-century Dutch coin of the VOC (*right*)

desertion of a Dutch officer of Danish origin, Jan de Hornay, who had married a Timorese, further weakened the presence of the Netherlands in the region.

Only in 1636, when the Dutch again expelled the Portuguese from Solor island, did the Dominican friars settle permanently in Timor. At that time, they were still primarily working in the western part of the island in Kupang and Oecussi. In 1641, the Dominicans reinforced their position though the conversion to the Catholic faith of several kings and queens in the kingdoms of Lifau, Mena, Amarante, Amanubau, Batimião, and Sonba'i. The same year, the VOC attacked Malacca, driving the Portuguese out and obliging them to settle in Makasar, and then Timor.

In 1642, with the help of soldiers from their newly converted allies, the Portuguese launched an expedition against the powerful kingdoms of Waiwiku-Wehale, which they managed to overthrow.

Nicolas Petit, 1801. Private collection

Timorese apparel at the beginning of the nineteenth century

Timorese warriors

Corn harvest in the Marobo area

Chapter 5

THE RISE OF THE PORTUGUESE
AND TOPASSES, 1641–1769

Overview

Topasses were mixed-blood Timorese with Portuguese or other European ancestry living in Lifau (Oecussi). Starting in the mid-seventeenth century, they gained power over some of the historical kingdoms. From 1673 to 1693, António de Hornay was described as virtual king of Timor. The Topasses valued their links to Portugal, but they did not want a governor imposed on them from the outside.

Around 1710 the Portuguese introduced the *finta*, a tribute to be paid by each kingdom. This led to many rebellions. In the 1760s, the Topasses killed Dutch and Portuguese representatives in Timor. In 1769, the Portuguese governor was forced to leave Lifau, and he founded a new capital at Dili.

5.1 The rise of the Topasses, 1642–1702

In 1642, the victory over the kingdom of Waiwiku-Wehale helped to increase the prestige of Portugal as well as of the Catholic faith. In 1645, the Dominicans began building a fort in Kupang. A vicar general was appointed to Timor in 1646. Other religious orders also settled for a few decades in Timor: the Jesuits in 1658 in Motael in the vicinity of Dili, and the Franciscans in 1670 in Manatuto.

Meanwhile, the Dutch were trying to expel the Portuguese from Southeast Asia. In 1652, they seized Kupang, forcing the Dominicans to move their main base to Lifau. In 1661, the Portuguese agreed to sign a treaty with their Dutch rivals. The VOC recognized the sovereignty of Portugal on the island of Solor and on the major part of the island of Timor. In return, the Portuguese agreed to acknowledge the Dutch presence in Kupang.

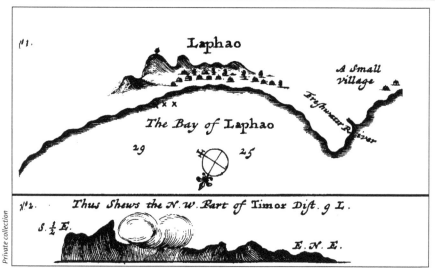

Map 20: Map of Timor and sketch of Lifao (Lifau) Bay, by William Dampier, 1699

This period saw the strengthening of Topass or "Black Portuguese" leaders, those who were from the community of mixed-blood Portuguese (or other Europeans) and Timorese. There were two main families, the de Hornay descendants of the Danish deserter Jan de Hornay, and the da Costa family of Portuguese origin.

From 1673 to 1693, the Topass António de Hornay took control of most of the Lesser Sunda Islands, including Flores, Solor, and Timor. As *capitão-mor*, he has been called the virtual king of Timor. A few years later, in 1695, an envoy of the Portuguese viceroy in Goa, António de Mesquita Pimentel, was deposed by the Topass Domingos da Costa. Domingos was also regarded as the king of Timor. Between 1693 and 1722, he chose alternatively to ally with or to oppose the Portuguese. In an attempt to reconcile, the Portuguese made him their governor from 1715 to 1718.

English navigator William Dampier, who stayed in Timor for almost three months in 1699, describes the ambivalence of the Topasses, who were very proud of their alliance with the Portuguese but would not consent to being governed by foreigners:

> The natives seem in words to acknowledge the King of Portugal for their Sovereign. Yet, they will not accept any Officer sent by him.
>
> The inhabitants of Lifau speak Portuguese and are of the Catholic religion. They value themselves on the account of their religion and descent from Portuguese; and would be very angry if a man should say they are not Portuguese. Yet, I saw but three White Men, two of which where Padres. There are also a few Chinese living here.
>
> Their common subsistence is by Indian corn, which every man plants for himself. They have a few boats and some fishermen. Their arms arc lances, thick round short truncheons and targets. With these, they hunt and kill their game and their enemies too, for this island is now divided into many kingdoms and all of different languages; though in their customs and manner of living, as well as shape and color, they seem to be of one stock. (Dampier 1981, 176–77)

Captain Dampier confirms that the island was divided into many independent kingdoms. Portuguese influence was important from a cultural point of view, but also economically, especially through the importation of corn from South America, which had become the dominant food crop.

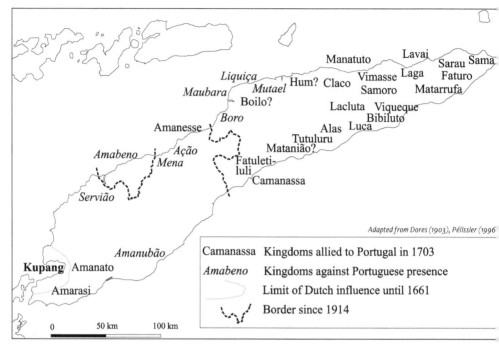

Map 21: The kingdoms of Timor according to Portuguese governor Coelho Guerreiro, 1703

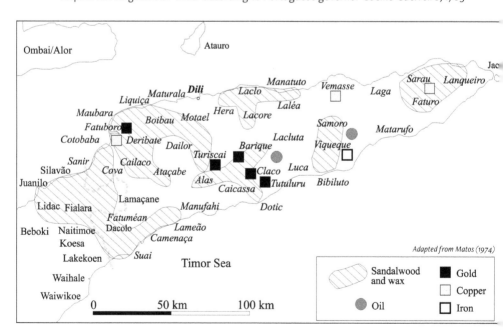

Map 22: Commodities for trade in Timor at the beginning of the eighteenth century

5.2 The strengthening of the Portuguese presence and the first major uprisings, 1702–1726

Portugal sent its first governor to Timor in 1702, António Coelho Guerreiro. He spent three years in Lifau before he was forced to flee because of repeated attacks by the Topasses led by Domingos da Costa. During those years, Coelho Guerreiro compiled a list of kingdoms, or *reinos*, that were known to the Portuguese, including twenty-five *reinos* allied with Portugal and nine that rejected Portuguese influence. By comparing this list to Erédia's map of 1613, we have evidence that the Portuguese were moving eastward. From then on, the Portuguese were aware of most of the coastal kingdoms in eastern Timor. They bought their agricultural products (corn, sago, rice) and other resources (gold, copper, oil). In western Timor, António Coelho Guerreiro could only identify eight kingdoms. Guerreiro left two maps, one of the bay of Lifau and another of the fortress (*fortaleza*) that protected the beach at the foot of the hill.

Planta da praia de Baboo

Map 23: Sketch of Lifau Bay by Guerreiro

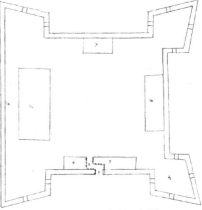

Planta da fort.ª da praya de Liphao de 200 pés
Portug.ᵒˢ de poligono exterior

Map 24: Plan of the Portuguese fort in Lifau by Guerreiro

During his stay Guerreiro set up two systems that had a long-term effect on relations between the East Timorese and the Portuguese: the awarding of military rank and the payment of the *finta*.

The allocation of Portuguese ranks such as colonel or commander or captain garnered the support of many local leaders. However, unlike initial relations that were established on symbolic alliances, trade, and commerce, the introduction of the *finta* was deeply resented by many Timorese kings and led to numerous wars. The *finta* was a sort of tax or in-kind tribute that allied kings were obliged to pay to the Portuguese governor in the form of, for example, sandalwood, honey, gold, or food.

The most famous wars of this time began in 1719, under the command of Topass leader Francisco de Hornay. In 1726, fifteen kingdoms from Oecussi to Ermera allied against the Portuguese. Meanwhile, the Portuguese managed to get the support of the majority of *reinos* from the easternmost part of the island. Thus, the conflict covered the major part of what constitutes Timor-Leste territory today.

The battle of Cailaco, which ended the war, lasted a month and a half, from October 23 to December 8, 1726. Fifty-five hundred men joined up from among the allies of Portugal, with probably as many on the opposing side.

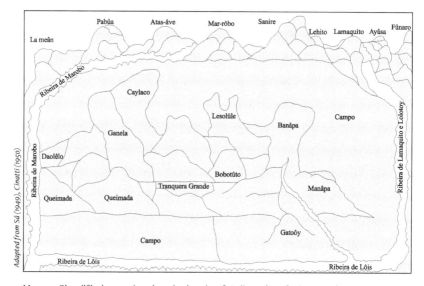

Map 25: Simplified map showing the battle of Cailaco (see facing page)

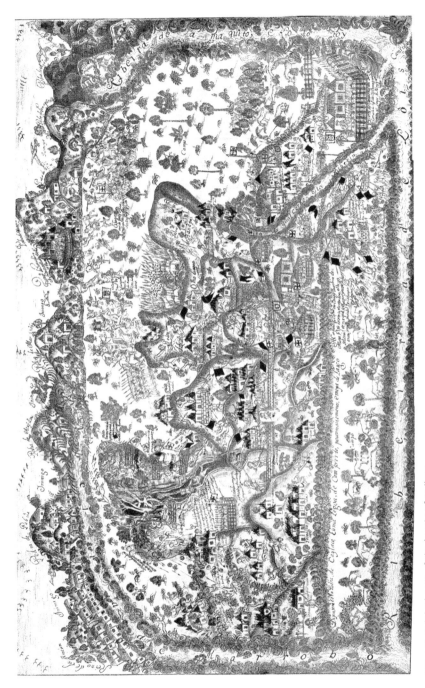

Map 26: Original map of the battle of Cailaco

Some fights were of a rare violence, as evidenced by the drawings of assaults and destroyed villages on a map commemorating the battle. But nature finally took over. By early December, heavy rains had forced the Portuguese troops to withdraw to Dili, which served as the base of the expedition.

The Cailaco campaign had no real winner. However, it demonstrated the power of the Portuguese to act and mobilize. A few years later, in 1733, a list of kingdoms agreeing to pay the *finta* shows that all of those in eastern Timor, including some in the interior, acknowledged the Portuguese crown.

5.3 The decline and resurgence of the Topasses, 1726–1769

Relations between Timorese and foreigners remained ambivalent after the battle of Cailaco. The Topasses welcomed the opening of a Catholic seminary in Oecussi by the Dominicans but at the same time tried to get rid of the Dutch. In 1749, the Topass of Portuguese origin Gaspar da Costa led a force estimated at fifty thousand men to the plain of Penfui, near Kupang. The Dutch commander had only twenty-three European soldiers and a few hundred former slaves or warriors of the islands of Savu, Roti, and Solor. Despite the imbalance of forces, the battle turned in favor of the Dutch. According to figures given by the VOC, two thousand Topasses might have died with their allies in the fighting and debacle that ensued.

The Dutch tried to take advantage of this victory by launching a series of military expeditions in the 1750s. At the same time, they sent an envoy, Johannes Andreas Paravicini, to negotiate new alliances with the kingdoms of the interior. His efforts culminated in the signing of the Treaty of Paravicini on June 9, 1756. Through this treaty, the Dutch extended their alliance by sealing agreements with fifteen new kingdoms in the southwestern part of the island.

These alliances were relatively formal and did not cover a continuous territory, since many important kingdoms in the west, such as Takaip and Insana, were not included. However, the symbolic dimension was strong. The most ambiguous aspect of this treaty was certainly the signature of the king of Wehale, previously an ally of the Portuguese. Without informing anybody, this king brought with him twenty-nine other kingdoms from central Timor. Yet those twenty-nine kingdoms had only acknowledged the religious and

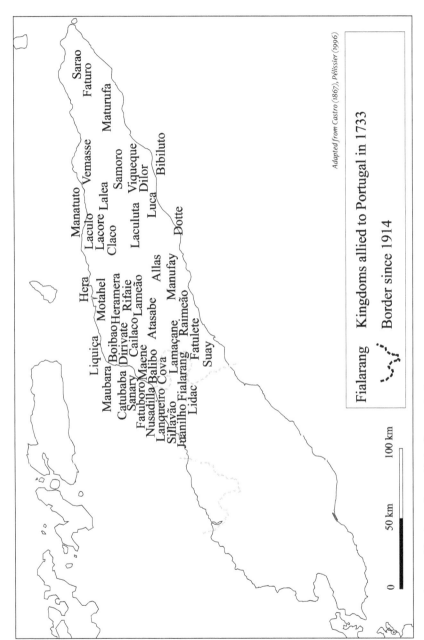

Adapted from Castro (1867), Pélissier (1996)

Fialarang   Kingdoms allied to Portugal in 1733

Border since 1914

0   50 km   100 km

Map 27: Timorese kingdoms that paid the *finta* to the Portuguese, 1733

moral authority of Wehale and were not his political vassals. Furthermore, fourteen years later, in 1770, the king of Wehale agreed to take the title of colonel proposed by the Portuguese. Clearly, allegiances could be challenged.

Paravicini's successor, von Plüskow, tried to further extend the Dutch conquest. In 1759, he destroyed a stronghold of the Topasses in Animata. He then attacked the *tranqueira* of Noemuti, where he took four hundred prisoners and captured fourteen cannons. As a result, seven new kings of western Timor, who were formerly allied with Portugal, signed a treaty with the Dutch company.

Timorese warriors in a parade

Photo Ruy Cinatti

Timorese warriors rallying

At this point in history the Portuguese settlement might have disappeared. Indeed, threatened by the Topasses, the Portuguese governor Sebastião de Azevedo e Brito had sought refuge in Kupang. From a position of strength, von Plüskow proposed signing a tripartite agreement with Portugal, the VOC, and the Topasses. He went to Lifau in 1761 but was killed by Francisco de Hornay and António da Costa, the descendants of the two former rival Topass families, who had decided to join forces. For the next century, apart from taking Atapupu in 1818, the Dutch stayed in Kupang and scarcely ventured into the interior of Timor.

Topass leader Francisco de Hornay, supported by his mother Dona Agostinha, then resumed his attacks on the Portuguese colony of Lifau. In 1766, Governor Dionísio Rebelo Gonçalves Galvão was killed by the Topasses. The blockade they set around the Portuguese settlement led to a food shortage. The new governor, António Teles de Menezes, arrived in 1768. Given the situation, he made the decision to move the capital to the east. On August 11, 1769, the population loyal to the Portuguese, altogether twelve hundred people, half of them women and children, left by boat to settle in Dili, leaving the Oecussi region to the Topasses.

Wedding in Timor

Private collection

Chapter 6

ALLIANCES AND CONFRONTATIONS IN EASTERN TIMOR, 1769–1852

Overview

From 1769 to the early 1850s, the Portuguese encountered many difficulties in their relations with the kingdoms of the eastern part of Timor, which were less familiar than the western kingdoms. In the early nineteenth century, attempts at coffee cultivation and exploitation of natural resources were not very successful. At the same time, the Catholic orders were being driven out of Timor by the king of Portugal.

In 1851, facing a very precarious financial situation, the Portuguese governor Joaquim Lopes de Lima agreed to recognize the sovereignty of the Netherlands over most of the Lesser Sunda Islands and over the western part of Timor.

6.1 Dili, a fragile new center for the Portuguese, 1769

Portuguese governor António Teles de Menezes took two months to navigate from Lifau to Dili, where he founded his new capital on October 10, 1769. On his way, he stopped at Batugade in order to strengthen the fort so that the Topasses could not pursue him eastward.

For the Portuguese, it was a new start. They knew less about the eastern part of the island than the western part, although the Jesuits had been established in Motael for some decades during the previous century. In 1769, forty-two East Timorese kingdoms recognized the authority of Portugal. The governor took the opportunity to strengthen his power at the expense of the religious orders, with mixed effects. In early 1770, he withdrew permission for the Dominicans to make inter-island trade of sandalwood, depriving them of what had been their main source of income for two centuries. This

Scene from daily life in Dili, 1818

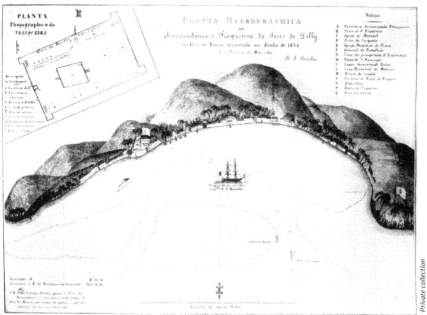

Map 28: Sketch of Dili Bay by Portuguese cartographer B. I. Bothelo, 1834

measure might have prompted the missionaries to support a Timorese revolt in Manatuto in 1778. It is also likely that the extension of the *finta* system to the east and the creation of a customs service in Dili caused new protests. From 1779 to 1810, the kingdom of Luca on the southern coast confronted Portugal in what was called the "War of the Mad" (*Guerra dos Doidos*). At the end of this period, the fight was led by the queen Dona Maria. Strengthened by their ability to resist, the Timorese tended not to resume their allegiance to the crown of Portugal. In 1810, only sixteen Timorese kingdoms continued to pay the *finta*.

To make up for this loss of income from the colony, the Portuguese began coffee cultivation in 1815, but without much initial success. Exploration for oil in the late 1810s and for metals in the early 1830s was also unsuccessful. In 1844, the transformation of Dili into a "free port" with limited duty had little effect and hardly improved the situation.

Meanwhile, in 1834, King Pedro IV decided to ban all religious orders in Portugal and overseas territories. The Dominicans and other priests were expelled from East Timor and Father Gregório Maria Barreto became the first Timorese priest to lead the clergy of East Timor. In 1856, he conducted the first census of the East Timorese Catholics. They numbered 6,124, or approximately 2 percent of the population.

6.2 The first border delimitation, 1851–1852

In the early 1850s, the island of Timor was far from being colonized. In the western part, the Dutch remained stationed in Kupang and Atapupu, with a force of only fifty soldiers. Their activity was limited to the collection of sandalwood brought by Chinese merchants, who were venturing into the island's interior. In the eastern part, despite some attempts at controlling the local trade and kings, the Portuguese colony of Dili remained an enclave in the middle of kingdoms that scarcely accepted intrusions and were quick to take up arms.

Despite this less than favorable context, the Dutch proposed to the Portuguese that they delineate the border between the two territories that each considered to be their colony. Up until then, no boundaries had ever been drawn between Dutch and Portuguese territories in Timor, and the status of other Lesser Sunda islands was still pending. It was in this context that the Dutch offered to delimit the frontier between the two territories for the first time, as well as to rule on the status of other islands in the Lesser Sundas. A new Portuguese governor, Joaquim Lopes de Lima, who arrived in Timor in June 1851, was responsible for the negotiation. Discovering a deplorable financial situation, he agreed to sign a tentative treaty whereby Portugal would renounce its claims on former Portuguese territories in Flores, as well as on the islands of Solor, Adonara, and Lomblem, against an offer of two hundred thousand guilders and the transfer to Portugal of the Dutch enclave of Maubara.

Lopes de Lima agreed to draw the boundary line in central Timor, although the status of many areas remained ambiguous and disputable.

Private collection

Portuguese governor Joaquim Lopes de Lima

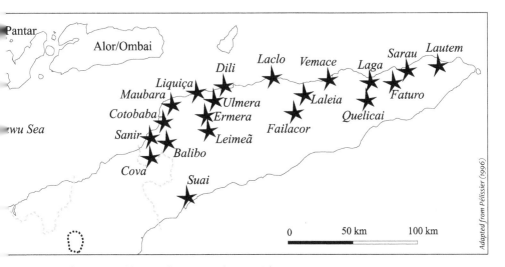

Map 29: Timorese uprisings against Portugal, 1847–1863

The Portuguese government refused to recognize the treaty, arguing that Lopes de Lima had overreached his mandate and had no authority to make such commitments. The governor was relieved of his duties and arrested in September 1852. All subsequent attempts at renegotiation failed, including a proposal from Portugal in 1858 to give the Dutch territories in Africa and to waive claims on all other Lesser Sunda islands, provided that the Dutch withdraw completely from Timor. The Treaty of 1851 was finally approved on April 20, 1859. But negotiations continued and the final demarcation of the border was not made for another fifty years.

E. Chabot after Wallace, in Wallace (1872). Private collection

Portraits of Timorese, 1859

Part 3

THE COLONIZATION OF THE MID-NINETEENTH CENTURY

Portrait of Portuguese governor Celestino da Silva on a Timorese banknote

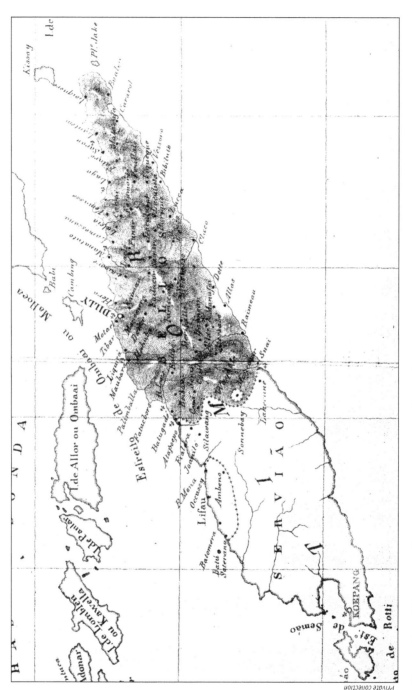

Map 30: Map of Timor according to Portuguese governor Affonso de Castro, 1867

Chapter 7

COLONIAL WARS OF THE SECOND HALF OF THE NINETEENTH CENTURY

Overview

In the 1860s, Governor Affonso de Castro took significant measures leading to the establishment of the first administrative division of East Timor and the extension of coffee cultivation through the imposition of forced labor.

The introduction of modern weapons helped the Portuguese overcome those Timorese kingdoms that continued to oppose control by a foreign power. This period marks the real beginning of Timor's colonization. Celestino da Silva, who was governor from 1894 to 1908, conducted many military campaigns, which also led to the creation of infrastructure.

7.1 Implementation of the colonial project from 1860

Governor Affonso de Castro, who held the governorship from 1859 to 1863, played a major role in changes that occurred in East Timor in the second half of the nineteenth century. He wrote the first book on the history of the country, *Portuguese Possessions in Oceania* (*As Possessões Portuguezas na Oceania*), published in 1867. He was also at the origin of political and administrative transformation, notably of the division of East Timor into eleven military districts, shaping the contemporary administrative boundaries and thereby encroaching on local powers. Faced with a critical financial situation from the overexploitation of sandalwood, Affonso de Castro also made decisions that were hard for the Timorese to accept. He increased the amount of the *finta* and introduced forced and statutory labor. As an adherent of the controversial system of forced cultivation established by the Dutch in Java in the 1830s, Affonso de Castro tried to oblige the Timorese to plant coffee and deliver 20

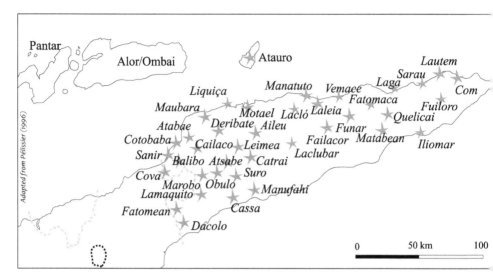

Map 31: Timorese uprisings against Portugal, 1867–1893

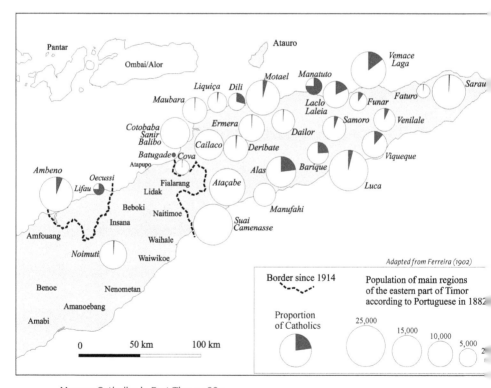

Map 32: Catholics in East Timor, 1882

percent of their harvest to the Portuguese authorities. Those who could not plant coffee would have to provide 10 percent of their food crop.

Only beginning with this epoch can we speak of the colonization of Timor. In fact the previous administrative system was mainly based on alliances or symbolic tributes. These new requirements led to renewed uprisings in the Timorese kingdoms, including Lacló, Maubara, Manatuto, and Laga. The insurgencies went on after the departure of Affonso de Castro, culminating with the assassination of Governor Lacerda e Alfredo Maia in 1887. The Portuguese began to import sophisticated weapons, which gave them a clear advantage over local populations. The repression became harsh.

These years were also marked by initial efforts to modernize the territory, such as awarding the status of city (*cidade*) to Dili in 1864, installation of the first library in Lahane (1879), construction of Dili's lighthouse (1881), introduction of street lighting in Dili using oil from Laclubar (1884), opening of the first public schools (mid-1880s), publication of prayer books in Tetum (1885), and creation of a regular sea link with Macao (1891).

However, Portuguese influence was still limited. The changes mainly affected the area around Dili and a minority of "assimilated" Timorese. A census of Catholics in 1882 indicates there were twenty-three thousand believers, or about 8 percent of the population.

Dili lighthouse, early twentieth century

The Catholic mission in Lahane, early twentieth century

Portuguese governor
Celestino da Silva

Carlos I, king of Portugal,
1863–1908

E. Chabot after Temmink, in Wallace (1872). Private collection

Engraving of a Timorese
warrior

Photo Ruy Cinatti

Timorese horsemen

Private collection

Company of *moradores* in Dili in the 1910s

Private collection

Company of *moradores* in Dili in the 1920s

7.2 The impact of Governor Celestino da Silva (1894–1908)

Since 1702 most of the Portuguese governors had stayed in Timor for less than two or three years, sometimes only for a few months. But Celestino da Silva showed exceptional longevity, holding his position for fourteen years, from 1894 to 1908. Da Silva was a former member of a cavalry squadron in which Dom Carlos I, the king of Portugal, had served. Throughout his mandate, Celestino da Silva benefited from the support of the sovereign, despite many criticisms of his actions in Timor, both economically and militarily.

In fact, Celestino da Silva was the first governor to deploy modern weapons on a large scale, namely, machine guns and grenades supported by gunboats. This enabled him to launch more than twenty military campaigns in fourteen years, in all regions of East Timor. The most renown campaign was against the powerful kingdom of Manufahi in 1895 and 1900 (see chapter 8), but he also launched numerous offensives in the west (for example, Atabae, Atsabe, Balibo, Cailaco, Fatomean, Marobo), in the extreme east (for example, Com, Fuiloro, Iliomar, Lautem, Matabean) and in Atauro in 1905.

Those campaigns gradually weakened the Timorese kingdoms. This had only been possible because of the ambivalence of some Timorese *liurais*, who had put their commitment to Portugal ahead of their desire for independence. Other leaders also feared retaliation and chose to take advantage of the military campaigns to conduct raids upon their neighbors. In general, the governor had only two hundred Portuguese soldiers and fifteen hundred *moradores* (local soldiers recruited in Dili). Without the support of the rulers, who led forces that sometimes exceeded ten thousand men, the Portuguese could not have overcome all the Timorese kingdoms.

Governor Celestino da Silva was also the initiator of a project to transform the *finta* into a head tax or capitation tax (1906), which had very serious consequences in the early 1910s. More broadly, Governor da Silva's main goals were to control the kingdoms and to increase his revenue by taxing land exchanges and promoting coffee cultivation.

His political approach consisted of two main objectives:

1) Maintaining alliances with the Timorese kingdoms while dividing and conquering;

2) Setting up a military and judiciary administration based on traditional rights, yet superimposing Portuguese law and authority.

To achieve these objectives, he established numerous forts served by a network of tracks and connected by telephone.

Governor da Silva also introduced positive changes, even if they were realized by using forced labor, namely, the drainage of Dili's marshes, the establishment of a water service in Dili, the installation of Canossian and Jesuit missions in Soibada in 1899, the creation of schools in the districts, the foundation of the agricultural company SAPT (Sociedade Agrícola Pátria e Trabalho), and the construction of a modern hospital in Dili in 1906.

At the end of da Silva's term in 1908, there were also three hundred kilometers of telephone lines in Timor, mainly for administrative and military use.

Dili hospital, around 1915

Canossian mission school for girls in Soibada in the 1930s

Chapter 8
THE MANUFAHI WARS, 1895–1912

Overview

The wars conducted against the Portuguese by the kingdom of Manufahi
illustrate the fierce resistance with which the Timorese opposed the
expansion of Portuguese influence and the difficulties that the Portuguese
soldiers faced in the late nineteenth century, despite their access to
modern weapons.

It took the Portuguese no less than three military campaigns spread
over more than fifteen years to subdue the kingdom of Manufahi.

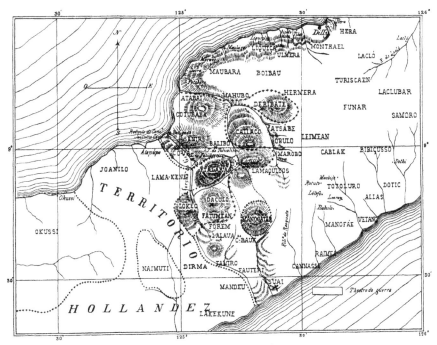

Map 33: Map of Portuguese military campaigns, 1895–1896

8.1 The first Manufahi campaign of 1895

By the end of the nineteenth century, Manufahi was a very powerful kingdom, with more than forty-two thousand inhabitants. In 1874 and again in 1894, the *liurai* of Manufahi, Dom Duarte Souto Maior da Costa, had recognized the sovereignty of the king of Portugal and offered to pay the *finta*, after not having paid it since 1860. Yet in 1895, Dom Duarte again refused to pay the *finta* and furthermore refused to provide the twenty men that Governor Celestino da Silva had requested as laborers. Dom Duarte replied that he was ready to continue trading and to welcome Catholic missionaries, but that he did not want to give up his independence.

Governor Celestino da Silva mustered a force of 22 officers, 350 *moradores*, and 12,000 Timorese warriors to oblige Dom Duarte to submit. To defend himself against the Portuguese, Dom Duarte united with other kingdoms, notably Raimean, Suai, Camenasse, Tutuloro, Liurai, and Letefoho (see map 33, with alternate spellings). In September 1895, he succeeded in destroying a column of several hundred Portuguese soldiers and seized many rifles as well as a dozen cannons.

The Portuguese sent three thousand men to Manufahi, but after fifty days of fighting, both sides had to withdraw because of the rainy season, leaving no real victor. Dom Duarte agreed, in principle, to pay the *finta* and accepted the establishment of a military post on his land. However, he refused to go to Dili to swear allegiance to the governor.

Agência geral das Colónias (1930). Private collection

Portuguese military post, early twentieth century

8.2 The second Manufahi campaign of 1900

In September 1900, Dom Duarte continued to engage in passive resistance. He had not paid his arrears of the *finta* nor did he allow the Portuguese to build a fort or lay tracks in his kingdoms. On the pretext of an attack in Manufahi against a Timorese king who was allied with Portugal, Celestino da Silva mustered an unprecedented force: 100 officers and NCOs, 1,500 *moradores*, 12,300 Timorese warriors, and 650 carriers. Altogether, the Timorese represented 99 percent of the military force available to the governor.

Divided into three columns, these armies went down to the south by the end of September 1900. On October 18, Maubisse was taken. On October 26, Letefoho fell. But it took more than four days of fighting to defeat Babulo. Celestino da Silva was impressed by the resilience and the pugnacity of the Timorese. The Portuguese managed to win the battles just because they had modern guns and grenades.

Meanwhile, Dom Duarte had entrenched himself with his men in Leo Laco, a hill covered with forest, that had been fortified by creating trenches, stone walls, and bamboo fences. Attacks and counterattacks lasted two weeks, from November 6 to 19, 1900, during which Manufahi's warriors managed to seize a Portuguese cannon.

The Portuguese troops were weakened by fighting, but also by smallpox and dysentery. As for Dom Duarte and his men, they were blocked on the top of the hill and were running out of water. But he knew that time was in his favor with the approach of the rainy season. After the failure of an ultimate Portuguese assault supported by fire from three cannons, Celestino da Silva realized that he could not win. In order not to lose face, he promised to have mercy on those who surrendered. On November 21, 1900, he returned to Dili without having managed to conquer the kingdom of Manufahi.

Although fragmentary, the archives suggest that Celestino da Silva might have led another campaign in 1907. In any case he returned to Europe in 1908 after the death of his protector, Dom Carlos I, the king of Portugal, without having been able to defeat Manufahi.

Portuguese governor Filomeno
da Câmara

Forced labor in East Timor during colonial times

Forced labor in East Timor during colonial
times

Timorese king Dom Boaventura
do Manufahi

Stamp of Timor as a Portuguese
colony, depicting the gunboat
Pátria

Depiction of
Timorese warrior
on the front cover
of the book *Timor:
Anteroom of Hell?*
(1930)

8.3 The Great War of 1911–1912

It was only in 1911–1912, that Governor Filomeno da Câmara, a successor of Celestino da Silva, led the difficult conquest of the kingdom of Manufahi. Relations between Timorese and Portuguese had continued to deteriorate after a series of problems. In 1910, the abolition of the monarchy in Portugal and the advent of the Republic had called into question the symbolic link between the *liurais* and the king of Portugal. Moreover, the transformation of the *finta* into a capitation tax and the increase in statutory and forced labor for public works or coffee plantations had put increasing pressure on the population. In addition, projects to register crop production and livestock presaged new burdens and constraints.

In reaction to these threats, Dom Boaventura Manufahi, the son of Dom Duarte, allied with the *liurais* of Camenasse and Raimean in 1911. On December 24, they attacked the fort of Same, killing a lieutenant and several Portuguese soldiers. They also cut the telephone lines. Other Timorese attacks forced the Portuguese to evacuate their military forts in Hatolia, Maubisse, and Ermera.

Frightened by the progress of Dom Boaventura, Filomeno da Câmara decided to arm the civilian population of Dili. He also concentrated his forces at three posts and appealed for reinforcements from Macao, Goa, and Mozambique. In a first phase, from the beginning of January to early February 1912, Filomeno da Câmara tried to regain Aileu but was routed by Timorese forces of more than fifteen *reinos*. The governor lost a cannon in the battle and had to retreat to Dili, where such panic broke out that civilians took refuge on a steamship in the port.

Their fortune changed, however, on February 6 with the arrival of the gunboat *Pátria*, followed by two ships bringing reinforcements from Goa and Mozambique. With fresh troops, Filomeno da Câmara launched his men into new battles on February 22, 1912. It was only by the end of March 1912, after many battles, that the Portuguese were able to overcome the kingdoms of Fato Berliu, Turiscain (Turiscai), and Bibiçuço. To the west in Atabae and Cailaco, many groups preferred to die rather than to surrender.

On many occasions, the governor expressed his admiration for the mobility and pugnacity of the Timorese, for their skill in the art of guerrilla warfare,

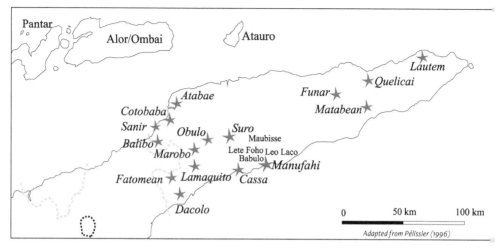

Map 34: Timorese uprisings against Portugal, 1894–1907

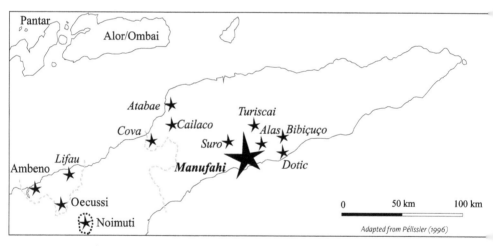

Map 35: Timorese uprisings against Portugal, 1908–1913

and for their ingenuity in using the military equipment that they had managed to seize from the Portuguese.

Luck would smile yet again on the Timorese. On March 22, 1912, João da Cruz Hornai, the Topass *liurai* descendant of the old de Hornay family, attacked the garrison of Pante Macassar, forcing the Portuguese to send a part of their troops into the enclave of Oecussi. Heavy fighting continued in many areas, including Ambeno, Maubisse, and Atsabe (Atabae). However, the arrival of two new steamers with troops from Mozambique in late April and mid-July tipped the balance in favor of the Portuguese.

In late May 1912, through the use of artillery, machine guns, and grenades, the troops of the governor were able to capture Aituto, where many warriors faithful to Manufahi had gathered, while the gunboat *Pátria* shelled coastal areas. The Timorese still had two strongholds, the *tranqueiras* in Riac and Leo Laco. From June 11 until July 21, 1912, Filomeno da Câmara besieged the fortress at the top of Riac. He was once again impressed by the inventiveness of the Timorese in using the topography to strengthen their defenses. It took forty days for the Portuguese to take Riac. They laboriously and repeatedly dug galleries to lay mines to blow up Timorese fortifications.

With Riac seized in July, only Leo Laco remained. Like his father twelve years before, Dom Boaventura had entrenched himself with more than twelve thousand men. The slopes of the hill had been drilled with holes in which soldiers were hiding. Natural defenses were reinforced by stone walls to protect the *tranqueira* at the top of the hill. On August 10, 1912, after being besieged for two weeks, Dom Boaventura was informed that new troops

Catálogo da Exposição (1939)

Timorese king going to a ceremony held by the Portuguese governor. Painting by Fausto Sampaio, 1937

were arriving from Mozambique. He therefore decided to attempt a crossing in force. He opened a breach in the Portuguese lines and managed to escape with several thousand men. The next day, a second wave succeeded in breaking through Portuguese lines. The others died or were taken prisoner on August 11, 1912. Sporadic attacks continued until October 1912 and even until May 1913 in Oecussi-Ambeno. But the balance of power had now shifted in favor of the Portuguese.

Overall, the fighting of 1911–1912 resulted in the deaths of fifteen thousand to twenty-five thousand East Timorese, or over 5 percent of the population at the time. Although doubts remain, the Portuguese probably did not manage to capture Dom Boaventura and João da Cruz Hornai. Nevertheless, the Timorese kingdoms had been seriously weakened. In addition, the show of force had led to the resignation of most local leaders and to the acceptance of the colonial presence.

It is worth mentioning that, in counterpoint, Filomeno da Câmara was the first governor to try to promote Tetum, by editing textbooks for schools that welcome young Timorese. However, this initiative was abandoned by his successors.

Chapter 9

POLITICAL AND ECONOMIC TRANSFORMATIONS AND FINAL BORDER DEMARCATION

Overview

In the aftermath of the military campaigns, the second half of the nineteenth century and the early twentieth century saw the introduction of major changes in East Timor. The official demarcation of the border between the eastern and western parts of the island was only completed in 1914.

The Timorese leaders had seen their political authority gradually shrink, while the role of women in society also diminished. From 1860, the decline of sandalwood production and the rise of coffee led to important socioeconomic changes.

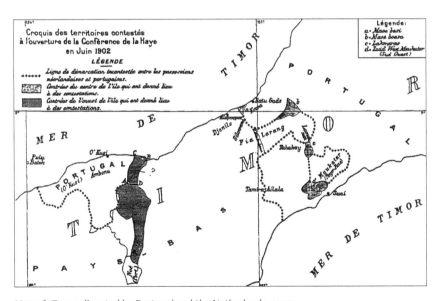

Map 36: Zones disputed by Portugal and the Netherlands, 1902

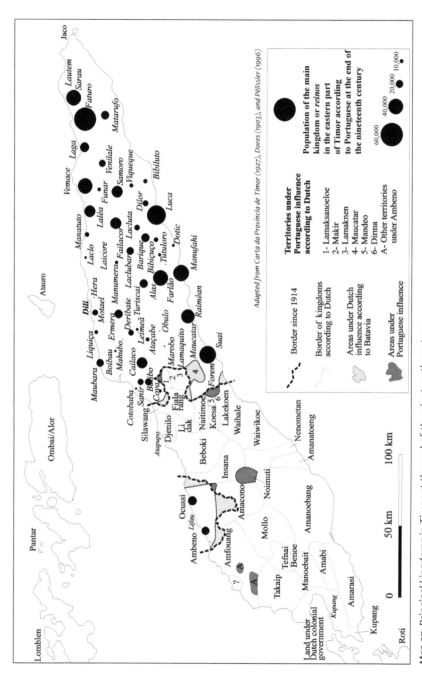

Map 37: Principal kingdoms in Timor at the end of the nineteenth century

9.1 The difficult border delimitation, 1893–1914

It was only in 1893, after the signature of an agreement in Lisbon, that Portugal and the Netherlands really began to worry about the precise demarcation of the border that they had negotiated in the 1850s.

It took several years before a joint commission of experts was sent to the field. For six months, from August 1898 to February 1899, Portuguese and Dutch officials sought to delineate the two "colonies." Governor Celestino da Silva, then still in charge, had to mobilize two thousand troops to protect the surveyors in areas that Europeans scarcely knew and where people were often hostile to interference.

In February 1899, a few exchanges of territory were considered in order to reduce the number of enclaves. It was suggested that the Dutch enclave in Maucatar would be handed over to Portugal in exchange for the territories of Noimuti and Tahakay. However, the main enclave of Oecussi-Ambeno would remain attached to Portugal. Still, four kingdoms continued to be claimed by both sides. A new joint committee in 1902, followed by an agreement signed in The Hague in 1904, was unable to settle the disputes.

Surveying resumed in 1908 and 1909, but both parties were forced to suspend their work because of disputes on which neither side wished to concede and because of complaints by the Topasses of Oecussi-Ambeno, who were angry that Noimuti would be given to the Netherlands.

The situation remained very tense for months. The Dutch even sent several hundred soldiers to the border where a skirmish erupted in July 1911. It was only with arbitration from the International Court of Justice in The Hague on June 25, 1914, that the issue could be settled. Yet new field surveys were again necessary in 1915 and the formal handover of the exchanged territories only occurred on November 1, 1916.

9.2 Social transformation and Timorese "aristocratic republics"

Timorese political structures have been greatly altered by contact with the Europeans. In the past, most kingdoms (*reinos*) had two leaders: one was in charge of the local community, including their contact with the forces and spirits of nature; the other took care of external relations with other kingdoms. Initially, the first one was much more important. With the arrival of the Portuguese, the relationship was gradually reversed.

According to Affonso de Castro, besides the king, there were three classes in Timorese societies:

> The first is that of the *datos* and officers, the second corresponds to the ordinary people—freemen or commoners, and the third class is that of "slaves." Prisoners of war, sorcerers, and individuals captured from neighboring kingdoms sustain the system of slavery. Any slave can obtain his freedom by asking the king to pay the *finta*. There is a uniqueness about it. If the slave who achieves freedom belonged to a commoner, he rises from slavery to the second class of the society, but if his master was from the first class, then the slave becomes a nobleman or *dato*. (Castro 1867, 175)

Thus, the traditional slavery in Timor was not to be compared with what Arabs or Europeans practiced in Africa, as it was a temporary and less harsh status. The so-called slaves were more like dependents and generally treated as members of the family. Indeed, traditionally, a master could not give or sell his dependent to someone outside the island of Timor. Under European influence, those rules were no longer respected, and the status of slaves worsened until 1858, when slavery was officially abolished by Portugal.

The *liurais* ruled over kingdoms or *reinos* consisting of dozens of villages (*sucos*), which were themselves divided into hamlets (*aldeias/povoações*). In the mid-nineteenth century, the most important *reinos* could count up to 70,000 inhabitants (Motael) and even 130,000 (Maubara). However, most of them ranged between 2,000 and 30,000 inhabitants and fluctuated over time.

The kings or *liurais* had limited powers. In the 1860s, the Portuguese governor Affonso de Castro wrote:

> The real authority lies in the hands of *datos* [leaders of *sucos*], who are considered the masters of the land. Cases when the king may decide without consulting the council of *datos* are few. Not only does the king

consult the *datos*, but he is also obliged to submit to their deliberations. We can say that the kingdoms of Timor are "aristocratic republics."

This term, "aristocratic republic," is significant. In fact, *liurais* were traditionally elected by the dignitaries or noblemen (*datos*) based on the dual criteria of lineage and skills. Important decisions were taken by the council of *datos*. However, through contact with the Portuguese, the sense of hierarchy was modified and became more top-down and authoritarian, notably by the award of military ranks. The *liurais* were granted the rank of colonel, while the *datos* were made commander, captain, or sergeant.

From the eighteenth century on, the Portuguese governors sought to impose their right to "confirm" the appointment of the *liurais* via a system of "patents." Portuguese patriarchal traditions and male domination in the administration led to a decline in the role of women in the society. When a woman was named "colonel-queen," the governor requested the appointment of a male regent.

Before the 1860s, governors had not intervened much in the internal affairs of kingdoms. Their role was mainly to convince the kings to pay the *finta* and to provide warriors when other leaders challenged the Portuguese crown. After the wars of the second half of the nineteenth century and especially after those of Manufahi from 1895 to 1912, many rebel *datos* and *liurais* were killed or captured and removed from power. The Portuguese then increased their control over the kingdoms. They forced their leaders to become administrators and tax collectors for the colonial administration. Celestino da Silva also removed the *liurais'* control over the non-cultivated lands. While they used to have the power to

Private collection

The queen of Camenasse kingdom in the 1920s

allocate this land to the population, they lost this right when the lands were designated as state property.

9.3 The decline of sandalwood and the rise of coffee cultivation

The second half of the nineteenth century also brought changes in the economy of East Timor. Until the 1850s and 1860s, the transport of exports was relatively diverse and included Chinese traders, whalers, and Australian vessels seeking supplies. Timor provided them with its major products: sandalwood, beeswax, and honey, as well as food, horses, buffaloes, copra (or dried coconut meat), and "slaves." The commerce in slaves seems to have been relatively limited and was officially abolished in 1858.

The decline of sandalwood forests due to overexploitation had begun in the middle of the eighteenth century. By the 1850s, one century later, the economic importance of sandalwood had decreased significantly. Late protective measures proposed by Governors Celestino da Silva and Filomeno

Private collection

Family of coffee planters in the 1920s

da Câmara had no great effect and could not reverse the decline. Finally, a ban on cutting was instituted in 1926.

English and American whalers, which had showed up regularly, also became increasingly rare in the late nineteenth century due to a drastic reduction in the number of whales.

Given this context, coffee gradually became the mainstay of the economy. Beginning with a trial planting in 1815, coffee cultivation spread in the 1860s as large, private estates began using forced labor, and as *reinos* were forced to plant coffee trees in order to pay the *finta* and later the capitation taxes. Coffee exports rose from 10 tons in 1858 (4 percent of exports) to 150 tons in 1865 (roughly 65 percent of exports). Stimulated by the Portuguese, coffee production fluctuated between 800 and 2,600 tons from 1878 to the late 1930s. The main production areas were the mountains in the western part of the territory from Maubara to Ermera and Same.

Five patacas banknote, 1924

Private collection

Le café. Timor.

Portuguese engraving depicting the coffee trade in Timor

Agência geral das Colónias (1930). Private collection

Private collection

Infantry barracks in Dili, around 1910

Private collection

Dili port in the 1920s

Private collection

Dili city hall in the 1920s

The majority of the population continued to practice subsistence agriculture with corn, tubers, and rice, and over 95 percent of Timorese lived in rural areas. In fact, at the beginning of the twentieth century, the city of Dili itself had only a few thousand inhabitants.

Mineral resources, especially oil, had been prospected for in East Timor by British and Australian companies in the 1910s and 1920s, but at the time, none of the territory was found to be commercially exploitable.

Map 38: Map of Dili, 1927

Construction of the Dili cathedral in the 1930s

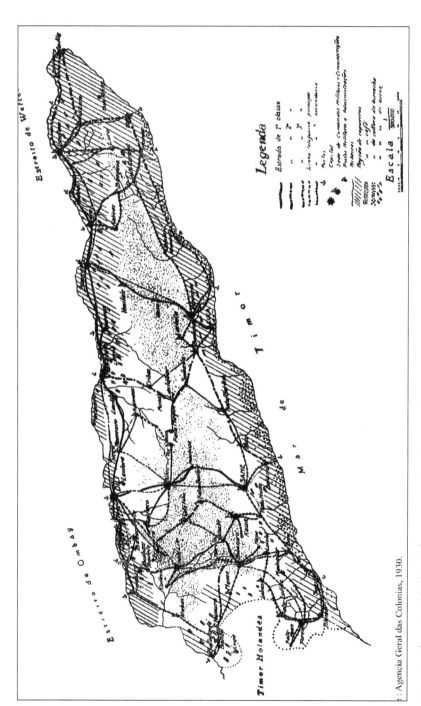

: Agencia Geral das Colonias, 1930.

Map 39: Main communications infrastructure in East Timor during the 1930s

Part 4

THE END OF THE COLONIAL PERIOD: 1941–1975

Portrait of Timorese king Dom Alexio Corte Real on the one hundred escudos banknote

Chapter 10

WORLD WAR II AND THE JAPANESE OCCUPATION, 1941–1945

Overview

Despite the neutrality of Portugal, Australian and Dutch soldiers entered East Timor in December 1941 to prevent the Japanese army from attacking Australia. The Japanese army invaded Timor in February 1942. Local people helped the Western forces until early 1943, when conditions became too difficult and the soldiers fled to Australia, along with some European civilians. The *liurai* of Suro, Dom Alexio Corte Real, distinguished himself in the struggle before being captured and executed.

Repeated bombings, fighting, and requisitions of men and food had tragic consequences. According to estimates, between 10 and 15 percent of the East Timor population died during those years.

Private collection

Timorese warriors and King Dom Alexio Corte Real (*fourth from left*) in the 1930s

10.1 A neutral Portugal between Western allies and Japan

The dictator António de Oliveira Salazar, who led Portugal from 1932 to 1968, pursued a policy of neutrality in international politics and the country and its overseas territories remained open. Australian oil companies had started exploration in East Timor in 1926. Meanwhile, some Japanese began settling in the territory in 1930. The Japanese were not only traders, but also investors, and they bought a 40 percent stake in the great agricultural company SAPT. In October 1941, Japan launched a shipping route to Dili via Palau. Beyond economical interests, the purpose was to store fuel and equipment in Timor, in view of the future war in the Pacific.

On December 7, 1941, Japan attacked the Americans at Pearl Harbor. Ten days later, Dutch and Australian troops numbering 1,100 men entered East Timor in spite of the neutrality of Portugal. Their goal was to ensure that Timor would not become a bridgehead for an invasion of Australia.

At that time there were only 150 Portuguese soldiers throughout the territory. In January 1942, President Salazar decided to send two boats from Mozambique with 800 men to defend Timor. However, the Japanese bombed Dili on February 8, 1942, before they arrived. Twelve days later they attacked the city. The Japanese army in East Timor grew to twenty thousand soldiers.

Private collection

Portuguese soldiers in East Timor in the 1930s

Portuguese forces withdrew to Aileu as they awaited reinforcements from Africa. Given the situation, on March 3 Salazar gave orders for the vessels to turn back. After having protested in vain against the violation of the neutrality of his country, the Portuguese governor Manuel de Abreu Ferreira de Carvalho had to accept this as fait accompli and establish a modus vivendi with the Japanese occupying forces.

10.2 World War II in East Timor

Australian and Dutch soldiers had retreated to the mountains before the arrival of the Japanese in February 1942. From there, they organized commandos to sabotage the invading army's facilities and equipment. They were only able to stand up to this army, numerically twenty times stronger than theirs, because of the help of local people. The East Timorese provided information to the Australians and allowed them to move and hide in areas where they could not have survived without assistance.

The Allies began bombing Dili from May 1942. Strategic targets included the telegraph station, power generators, warehouses, customs offices, and hospitals. With the destruction of the telegraph equipment, the governor was left unable to communicate with Portugal until the end of the war. The local population was also deprived of all these services. Meanwhile, the two opposing forces continued to drop their bombs over the whole territory. The principal victims were local people. Faced with these repeated bombings and abuse by Japanese troops, many Timorese protested against both the aggression of the Japanese army and the passivity of the Portuguese authorities.

In September 1942, the Japanese army established the "black columns" (*columnas negras*) to stop the revolts by the East Timorese and to weaken their support of the Australians. Largely composed of nationals from West Timor under Dutch jurisdiction, these militias sowed violence and destruction. In November 1942, the Japanese moved 600 Portuguese to camps in Liquiça and Maubara to better control them.

By December 1942, the Australians were facing increasing pressure and decided to evacuate their troops. They evacuated most of their men between

January and February 1943 from the southern coast of Timor. They also evacuated 540 Portuguese and mixed-race people, but left the Timorese people without defense. Japanese retaliations were particularly harsh towards those suspected of having helped Australian soldiers.

Many East Timorese distinguished themselves in the fight against the occupation. The *liurai* of Suro, Dom Alexio Corte Real, led intrepid operations against the black columns and the Japanese before being captured in May 1943 and executed.

The Japanese occupation went on under American and Australian bombings. Famines arising from the requisition of food and forced labor of men and women had drastic consequences for the population. Japanese troops also practiced seizures and stealing, including, in July 1944, seizing the financial reserves of the Banco Nacional Ultramarino (BNU). Furthermore, the Japanese administration in Timor attempted to impose its language and currency on the country.

Liurai Dom Alexio Corte Real, 1938

Carlos Cal Brandão's book *War in Timor* (1946). *Funo* means war in Tetum.

On August 6, 1945, the United States dropped a nuclear bomb on Hiroshima, followed by a second bomb on Nagasaki on August 9. On August 15, the emperor of Japan agreed to unconditional surrender. On September 5, the Japanese colonel Yoshioka met the governor of East Timor, Ferreira de Carvalho, to formally declare the end of the war and conduct an administrative restoration of sovereignty to Portugal. The Japanese command had previously ordered the destruction of the bulk of military equipment, including vehicles. The majority of Japanese troops were then moved to West Timor.

The Australian command, considering that it was "their" war, insisted that there be a second surrender, military this time. This surrender took place on September 24, 1945, although the Portuguese governor had resumed his duties almost three weeks earlier and only 110 Japanese soldiers remained in East Timor.

On September 27, 1945, two Portuguese ships arrived in Dili with 2,200 men, three engineering companies, food, and construction materials.

10.3 East Timor: An overlooked tragedy of World War II

In June 1946, an Australian commission was set up in Dili in order to investigate war crimes committed by the Japanese army between 1942 and 1945. Investigators were only interested in the deaths in the ranks of the Westerners and not among the local populations, which had paid the heaviest price. The Timorese had been caught up in the fighting between the Allies and Japan, both of which had disregarded the neutrality of Portugal and invaded the territory, strafing the towns and villages and killing tens of thousands of people.

Estimates indicate that between 45,000 and 70,000 East Timorese were killed during this period. It corresponds to between 10 and 15 percent of the local population estimated to be 450,000. As stated by former Australian consul in Dili, James Dunn:

> East Timor was one of the great catastrophes of World War II in terms
> of relative loss of life. Having in mind the human cost alone, Portuguese
> Timor suffered far worse than any other Southeast Asian country

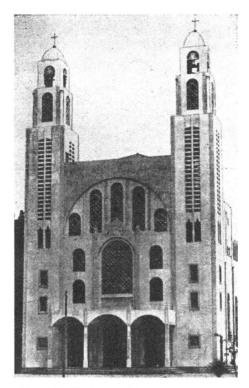

Dili Cathedral before World War II

Dili Cathedral, January 1946

occupied by the Japanese. Yet this aspect has never been properly acknowledged. It was as if the people of Timor were such shadowy and anonymous figures that Australians, who bore a heavy responsibility in the catastrophe, simply could not comprehend their suffering and pain. (Dunn 1983, 26)

By comparison to the tens of thousands of dead East Timorese, Australian losses are estimated at 40 men, those of Portugal, 75, and those of Japan, 1,500.

Material losses were also considerable. Over 90 percent of buildings were destroyed, including Dili's former grand cathedral. This is one reason why so few old administrative or religious buildings remain in East Timor. As James Dunn wrote:

Dili was mostly in ruins, having been bombed almost out of existence by the Allies, and the roads were impassable. The war seemed to have taken the country back to Stone Age. The task of reconstruction would have presented any colonial power with challenge. (Ibid.)

Chapter 11

THE "SUBMISSIVE" ALLIANCE BETWEEN TIMORESE AND PORTUGUESE, 1945–1974

Overview

The postwar reconstruction had been slow because the Allies excluded East Timor from war reparations.

Two events disturbed the territory in the 1950s and 1960s: the Viqueque uprising in June 1959 instigated by Indonesian refugees, and Indonesian incursions into the Oecussi enclave in August 1966. These troubles led to a hardening of the colonial regime.

Meanwhile, in 1960, the United Nations placed East Timor on the list of territories to be decolonized.

During this period, progress was made in education, agriculture, and the rehabilitation of roads, but the improvements were slow and modest.

Photo António Dias

The center of Dili in the 1960s

II.I The slow postwar reconstruction

Despite the magnitude of destruction and the suffering of its people, East Timor did not receive war reparations. As part of the San Francisco Conference of September 1951, the Western powers required Japan to pay compensation to the Southeast Asian territories that had been invaded. Even though they had not respected the neutrality of Timor, the Allies put aside Portugal's claims for its overseas territories, arguing—speciously—that East Timor and Portugal had not participated in the war.

East Timor therefore experienced a slow reconstruction, especially as the Salazar dictatorship led more and more Portuguese-speaking countries to relative autarky.

From May 27 to June 7, 1952, the Portuguese minister for overseas territories, Manuel Maria Sarmento Rodrigues, came to Timor as part of a journey to the Portuguese provinces of the Far East. It was the first time in four centuries of relations that a minister had visited Dili. He traveled to many regions, reaffirming the links between Portugal and Timor. He also awarded hundreds of medals to leaders and *liurais* who had distinguished themselves in the fight against the Japanese. Although the visit was very formal, the photos show a real popular mobilization.

Accounts by members of the delegation also show that, seven years after the end of World War II, much of Dili was still in ruins. Some delegates, however, were surprised by the agricultural wealth. They said it should not

Minister Manuel Maria Sarmento Rodrigues and schoolchildren, 1954

Minister Rodrigues awarding medals, 1954

take more than five or six years of proper planning before Timor could achieve a balanced economy that no longer depended upon Lisbon. The immense richness of Timorese culture was also noticed, with its languages, songs, costumes, rituals, and artifacts. The creation of a research center and of a museum of Timorese culture were considered, but the Portuguese government never put these ideas into concrete form.

Nevertheless, some steps were taken to improve the situation. The indigenous colonial status was abolished in 1953, giving the East Timorese full Portuguese citizenship. The number of primary schools rose from four in 1958 to thirty-one in 1962. This effort, however, remained insufficient in relation to needs, since only one-third of all children were enrolled in primary

Children in front of a Portuguese school in the 1960s

Photo Luis Filipe Thomaz

Portuguese health assistance in the 1960s

school. In the 1960s, three hospitals and fifty-one health posts scattered throughout the area had only twelve doctors and eighty-eight nurses. This made it difficult to meet the needs of a growing population, with an average population growth of 2 percent.

11.2 The Viqueque uprising of June 1959 and the incursions of August 1966

At the end of 1958, fourteen Indonesians fled their country and sought political asylum in Dili. They were said to be members of Permesta, a regionalist movement fighting against the excesses of centralism in Sukarno's government. The Portuguese governor authorized them to settle in Baucau and Viqueque. In March 1959, rumors began circulating implicating the Indonesian consul in Dili in the trouble. From June 7 to 20, 1959, a brief uprising erupted in the region of Viqueque, Uato Lari, Uato Carbau, and Baguia. This caused the death of five hundred to one thousand Timorese. The revolt also led to the arrest of sixty-five suspects. Those who were regarded as leaders were exiled to Africa.

The role and possible motivations of Indonesian factions in these events is unclear. Some see them as a first attempt to destabilize East Timor. Others consider them to be the first nationalist movement in the postwar period. In any case, it is certain that this unrest had an impact on the political awareness of the East Timorese. In 1974–1975, both the supporters of independence and the supporters of integration with Indonesia presented the Viqueque uprising as a source of inspiration for their opposing movements.

Another event suggests an underlying desire to destabilize East Timor. In August 1966, in the context of the end of the military confrontation between Indonesia and Malaysia (1963–1966), Indonesian troops entered the enclave of Oecussi-Ambeno under cover of a topographic mission, arguing over problems about border delimitation. This provoked violent responses by neighboring populations. Beginning in November, several villages were burned, notably around Passabe, where a military post came under mortar attack by the Indonesian army. However, with rapid military action the Portuguese governor put an end to the incursions. It could have been a preview of the invasion of December 1975, which was preceded by sporadic attacks in the same enclave.

In any case, in 1968, after a stint in East Timor, the Australian journalist Gert Vondra felt the tensions. He wrote in quite a prophetic way:

> Timor is rich in coffee, copra and natural resources. The territory produces honorable quantities of rice, rubber, groundnut . . . There is oil in Timor. But investors are reluctant because the political future is unclear. Maybe in the next few years, Indonesia will seize the administration of the territory, with or without UN sanctions. Or, the few educated Timorese will raise their voice and bring the Portuguese to give them autonomy in the management of their territory. (Vondra 1968, 103–4)

11.3 The tightening of colonial control

The Viqueque uprising in 1959 led to more political restrictions, including the installation in East Timor of Salazar's political police, PIDE (*Polícia Internacional e de Defesa do Estado*). The Salazar dictatorship probably felt even

Private collection

Table of contents of the April 1958 issue of *Seara* newspaper

Photo António Dias

Photo António Dias

Enrollment of young Timorese in the 1960s

more threatened on December 14, 1960, when the United Nations placed East Timor on the list of territories to be decolonized. The newspaper *Seara*, published bimonthly by the Diocese of Dili, was banned by the political police in March 1973. It had begun publication in 1948 and was East Timor's first newspaper. *Seara* was regarded as subversive because it allowed such future nationalists as Francisco Xavier do Amaral, Nicolau Lobato, Xanana Gusmão, José Ramos Horta, Mari Alkatiri, and Mário Carrascalão to express their views in its columns.

In counterpoint, it should be noted that during the years 1960–1974, Portugal made some efforts to improve the situation in East Timor, although they may be regarded as very modest. By the mid-1960s the Portuguese, even before the Indonesians in Java, had begun to import high-yield rice seeds from Institute of Los Baños in the Philippines to start a "green revolution." In 1969, encouraging results were obtained around Viqueque. It is from this period that tourism began to be perceived as a potential economic asset.

In the years 1960–1970, oil discoveries also revived the Portuguese interest in Timor. From 1972, the Portuguese government significantly increased its funding in the territory. Investments rose from US$1.2 to 5.1 million, from 1972 to 1973. Plans were also made to build 400 km of roads and to rehabilitate five airports.

Chapter 12

POLITICAL AWAKENING AND FAILURE OF THE DECOLONIZATION PROCESS, 1974–1975

Overview

The Carnation Revolution in April 1974 spawned political life in East Timor. By May 1974, several parties had been founded. The major ones, the UDT (Timorese Democratic Union) and the ASDT/Fretilin (Social Democrat Timorese Association/ Revolutionary Front for the Independence of Timor-Leste), favored independence.

Portuguese politicians, tempted at first by the option of allowing Indonesia to invade East Timor, finally set up a process of decolonization with a detailed timetable for independence.

The Indonesian secret service put pressure on some UDT leaders to take power by force. The subsequent coup d'état of August 1975 caused between fifteen hundred and three thousand deaths.

From September to early December 1975, Fretilin took control of the territory. The International Red Cross and many Western observers praised its administration and serious commitment to solving problems. Faced with the threat of invasion from Indonesia, Fretilin leaders declared independence on November 28, 1975.

12.1 The catalytic impact of the Carnation Revolution

In April 1974, the Carnation Revolution in Portugal—a coup without bloodshed against the dictatorship and the colonial system—ended the regime of Marcelo Caetano, Salazar's successor. In Timor, it led to a political blooming. The echo of struggles in the Portuguese colonies in Africa in the 1960s had already encouraged the emergence of a national consciousness among the literate minority.

Two weeks after the fall of the Portuguese dictatorship, the East Timorese took advantage of this opening to form political parties, which had previously been banned. Three parties were created in May 1974: the UDT (Timorese Democratic Union); the ASDT (Social Democrat Timorese Association), later Fretilin (Revolutionary Front for the Independence of Timor-Leste); and Apodeti (Popular Democratic Timorese Association). The first two were in favor of independence, even if the UDT was proposing a longer transition period.

In June 1974, the widow of Dom Boaventura, the leader during the Manufahi war, enrolled in the ASDT, giving a special aura to this party. All observers agree that Apodeti, which supported union with Indonesia, only represented a very small minority.

The majority of East Timorese also wanted to preserve their symbolic link with Portugal. António de Almeida Santos, the minister of international coordination, had the opportunity to verify this. In October 1974, ten thousand people came to cheer him in Dili and to salute the Portuguese flag. This enthusiasm, however, fit poorly with Portugal's inclination to withdraw from its overseas territories, as it was facing serious domestic political turmoil. During this same month an Indonesian delegation was in fact visiting Lisbon.

Since his appointment in November 1974, the new governor of East Timor, Mário Lemos Pires, had witnessed the population's loyalty to Portugal, although he also noted the existence of a strong East Timorese identity. Despite divergences of opinion among Portuguese political leaders in

Crowd welcoming Portuguese minister António Almeida Santos, 1974

Lisbon, Portugal began to implement a process of decolonization, which was confirmed during the Macao conference in May 1975. On July 17, 1975, Portugal enacted a decree on the decolonization of East Timor. A timetable was set, with the election of a constituent assembly planned for October 1976.

12.2 East Timorese political convergence against external influences

Timorese women also tried to resume a political role by creating the OPTM (Popular Organization of Timorese Women). To better prepare the process of independence, the two main political parties of East Timor, the UDT and Fretilin, formed a coalition in January 1975. The Indonesian military did not appreciate the move because it was likely to compromise their plans. They therefore undertook several maneuvers.

Indonesian generals organized regular talks with the Portuguese throughout 1975: in London in March, in Hong Kong in June, in Jakarta in August, and in Rome in November. Indonesian negotiators tried to persuade Portugal to transfer to them its sovereignty over East Timor, or at least to authorize the Indonesian army to enter the territory. Although they failed to secure any such agreement, they maintained the illusion of a dialogue so that Portugal did not request intervention by the United Nations, even after Indonesia began to launch sporadic attacks in June 1975.

General Suharto also sought the support of President Gerald Ford during a visit to the United States in July 1975. He easily won approval by arguing

By-elections in East Timor, March 1975

that Fretilin was regarded as a "communist" party that could destabilize the region. The Americans had just lost the Vietnam War in April 1975 and feared the propagation of communism in Asia.

Finally, the Indonesian secret services decided to break the coalition between Fretilin and the UDT. In May 1975, they invited leaders of the UDT to meetings with officials and military to let them know that Indonesia would never accept the formation of an independent government made up of members of Fretilin.

On May 27, 1975, the UDT unilaterally put an end to the coalition. A week later, a brief intrusion in the Oecusse enclave by the Indonesian army confirmed to the army that no strong reaction was to be feared on the part of Portugal. It was therefore possible to increase the pressure on East Timor. At the end of July 1975, the Indonesian intelligence services again invited several UDT leaders to talks. They were told that unless a decisive action was done to brush aside Fretilin, Indonesia would launch a military invasion.

Mari Alkatiri, Rosa Bonaparte, and Nicolau Lobato, 1975

12.3 The civil war of August 1975

In this oppressive context, the leaders of the UDT felt that there was no other choice but to carry out a coup. On August 11, 1975, they seized weapons from the police. Governor Lemos Pires did not react. Yet, it would not have been difficult to regain control. Less than two hundred men took part in the UDT coup, while the governor had more than seventeen hundred soldiers. In a few days, Fretilin managed to rally a majority of the East Timorese population, who were shocked by the coup. Most Timorese soldiers drafted in the colonial army deserted with their weapons to join Falintil (National Liberation Forces

Armed men, August 1975

of Timor-Leste), the military wing of Fretilin. On August 27, Fretilin took over control of Dili, and by mid-September, Fretilin controlled most of the territory. Meanwhile, Portuguese governor Lemos Pires left Dili to take refuge on the island of Atauro.

These troubles led to fighting and excesses on both sides. They caused between 1,500 and 3,000 deaths, while about 10,000 people fled to West Timor from late August 1975, along with the leaders of the UDT and other parties.

This short civil war could have been used as a pretext for an invasion, especially since the political situation was also very unstable in Portugal. But the Indonesian military commanders were reluctant. Furthermore, they had a means of pressure that they probably overestimated: the capture of twenty-three Portuguese officers and three civilians. The Indonesian army had allowed them to cross the border in August 1975 before putting the officers in camps for almost one year. The Portuguese government refused to allow the Indonesian army to enter East Timor unless the hostages were released. While the civilians were quickly let go, the military hostages were only freed in July 1976 when Indonesia unilaterally annexed the territory.

From September to early December 1975, the International Red Cross and many NGOs and Western journalists testified to the seriousness and commitment of Fretilin members in managing economic and social problems to ensure the continued functioning of the territory under very difficult conditions.

23 PORTUGUESES SÃO MOEDA DE TROCA EM TIMOR

Article from the Portuguese newspaper *Expresso*, July 3, 1976:
"23 Portuguese traded off in Timor"

12.4 The Declaration of Independence on November 28, 1975

From September 1975, the Indonesian army stepped up systematic attacks on border towns, including Suai, Batugade, Maliana, and Balibo, where five Western journalists were killed on October 16, 1975. On November 24, Fretilin leaders appealed to the United Nations, requesting them to send a peacekeeping force, with no result. On November 27, the city of Atabae fell, paving the Indonesian army's way to Dili.

Since September, Fretilin had administered the whole territory, with the exception of the enclave of Oecusse and the island of Atauro, where the governor had taken refuge. Fretilin had continued to recognize the sovereignty of Portugal and to request that the process of granting independence be completed. With no reaction from Portugal, and facing the inevitability of a massive Indonesian offensive, Fretilin decided to unilaterally declare the independence of the Democratic Republic of Timor-Leste on November 28, 1975.

The first president was Francisco Xavier do Amaral, with Nicolau Lobato as prime minister. The purpose of this desperate act was to induce a reaction from the international community. Several states recognized the new republic, including China, Cuba, Vietnam, and the former Portuguese colonies, but not the United Nations or any Western power. On November 30, 1975, representatives from the UDT and the other political parties, now virtually

Francisco Xavier do Amaral (*table center*) at the Declaration of Independence, November 28, 1975

prisoners in West Timor, were forced to sign the so-called Balibo declaration calling for the incorporation of East Timor into the Republic of Indonesia.

On December 4, 1975, several East Timorese ministers—José Ramos Horta (foreign affairs), Mari Alkatiri (political affairs), and Rogério Lobato (defense)—left Dili to try to gain international support.

Francisco Xavier do Amaral (*third from left*), with Portuguese and Fretilin flags behind him, 1975

Nicolau Lobato at the Declaration of Independence, November 28, 1975

Part 5

FROM INDONESIAN OCCUPATION TO INDEPENDENCE, 1975–2002

Xanana Gusmão (*center*) with the main resistance leaders during the ceasefire of 1983

Indonesian tanks in Dili, December 1975

Falintil unit

Guerilla fighters crossing a river

Chapter 13
THE YEARS OF ARMED STRUGGLE, 1975–1989

Overview

The Indonesian army invaded East Timor on December 7, 1975. Despite using heavy weapons and deploying tens of thousands of soldiers, the invaders encountered a very strong resistance movement.

Military campaigns and the establishment of camps for civilians had deadly effects, while at the same time convincing the East Timorese that they had no other choice but to fight for independence.

13.1 The invasion of December 7, 1975

On December 7, 1975, at four o'clock in the morning, the Portuguese administrators in Atauro saw five warships headed for Dili, followed by nine aircraft and at least one submarine. Once this first wave of attack opened fire, other forces joined in. A total of twenty warships and thirteen planes attacked the city. Ten thousand soldiers participated in the assault. Assailants made no distinctions among the population, mistreating even those who waved Apodeti flags. The East Timorese poet Borja da Costa died on December 7, along with hundreds of his compatriots and Australian journalist Roger East.

On December 8, two corvettes left Atauro, taking away the last Portuguese administrators. This fact is important. It shows that, contrary to what has often been written, the Indonesian army did not invade East Timor *after* the departure of Portugal even though, on December 7, these boats apparently did nothing to prevent what was happening.

The fighting continued in Baucau on December 10, then two weeks later in Liquiça, Suai, Aileu, and Manatuto. The resistance was far stronger than what had been expected by the Indonesian army.

Reacting to these attacks, on December 12, 1975, the UN General Assembly "strongly deplored the military intervention of the Indonesian armed forces in East Timor." The UN assembly also requested the Indonesian government to stop "violating the territorial integrity of Portuguese Timor, and to withdraw its armed forces immediately from the territory to enable the people to freely exercise their right to self-determination." This request was reiterated and adopted unanimously by the Security Council of the United Nations on December 22, 1975 (Resolution No. 384).

Yet, no peacekeeping force was sent. A special envoy of the UN secretary-general, Vittorio Guicciardi, spent two days inside East Timor in January 1976. He said that he was prevented by the occupation from meeting with representatives of Fretilin.

Indonesian army landing in Dili, December 7, 1975

Indonesian army parachuting over Dili the same day

13.2 First military campaigns and holding camps

Deluded by its own propaganda, the Indonesian army calculated that the fighting would last less than fifteen days. In late December 1975, given the magnitude of the resistance, 15,000 additional soldiers had to be sent, bringing their number to 25,000 or one soldier for twenty-eight people.

The number of Falintil fighters then amounted to nearly 30,000 men, all of whom were familiar with the mountainous territory, while the progress of Indonesian troops was hindered by the poor roads and the onset of the rainy season. The behavior of the occupiers also aroused rejection from those who might have treated them favorably. Even members of the UDT who were supposed to have supported the integration policy with the Balibo declaration attempted a coup against the occupying army in April 1976.

By the end of 1976, the Indonesia army controlled only the main roads. A majority of the population had fled to the mountains. The number of Indonesian forces was then increased to 40,000 men. In August 1977, they attacked Falintil headquarters in the mountains, between Laclubar and Lacluta. The resistance was forced to abandon the centralized management of its activities and to ask the 450,000 East Timorese who were with them to return to the lowlands.

In September 1977, the occupation army decided to undertake decisive actions through a military campaign of "encirclement and annihilation" and through the internment of civilians in camps. The troops attacked the border area and the north coast, and pushed Falintil toward the east and the south coast. From mid-1978 to March 1979, they heavily shelled the two main bastions of resistance, Natarbora and Matabean mountain.

In August 1978, Francisco Xavier do Amaral was caught by the Indonesian army. On December 31, 1978, Nicolau Lobato, who had become the new Fretilin president and the second president of the Democratic Republic of Timor-Leste was killed along with many fighters. In February 1979, Mau Lear (António Carvarino) and Sa'he (Vicente dos Reis) also fell in turn.

By early 1979, only small groups of resistance remained in the territory. Xanana Gusmão was one of the few founding members of Fretilin who had managed to escape the occupying army.

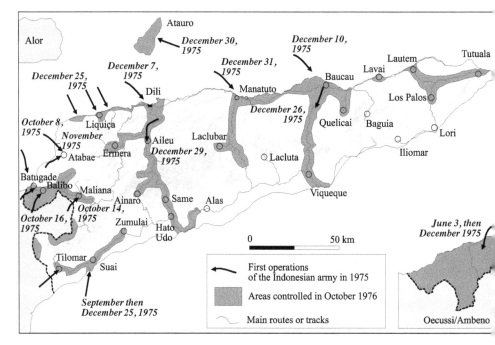

Map 40: Areas controlled by the Indonesian army at the end of 1976

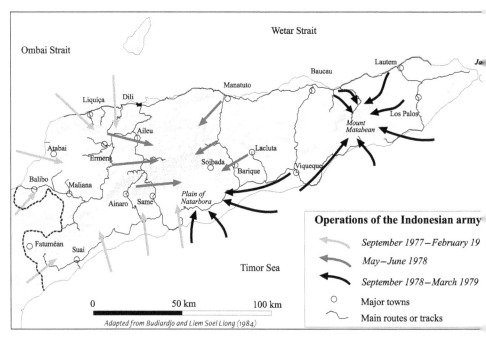

Map 41: The "encirclement and annihilation" campaign of the Indonesian military, September 1977–March 1979

The majority of civilians were sent to holding camps. According to the Indonesian army, in December 1978, 372,900 East Timorese, or 60 percent of the population, were placed in 150 camps. With very little land to cultivate, they experienced a famine that the International Red Cross considered to be "as bad as in Biafra and potentially as dramatic as in Cambodia." The situation did not improve in subsequent years. At least three other famines occurred in 1981–1982, 1984, and 1987.

Timorese refugees in the mountains, around 1977

Timorese children during the November 1979 famine

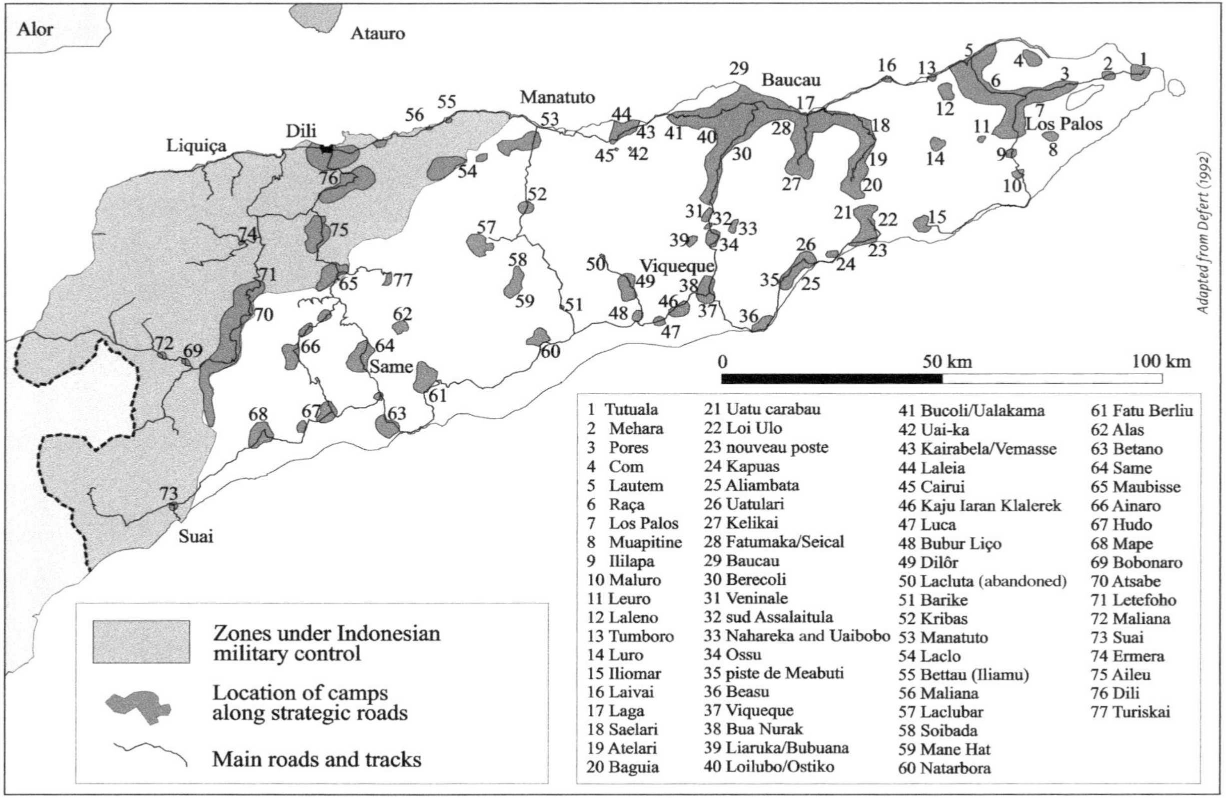

Adapted from Defert (1992)

0   50 km   100 km

1 Tutuala	21 Uatu carabau	41 Bucoli/Ualakama	61 Fatu Berliu
2 Mehara	22 Loi Ulo	42 Uai-ka	62 Alas
3 Pores	23 nouveau poste	43 Kairabela/Vemasse	63 Betano
4 Com	24 Kapuas	44 Laleia	64 Same
5 Lautem	25 Aliambata	45 Cairui	65 Maubisse
6 Raça	26 Uatulari	46 Kaju Iaran Klalerek	66 Ainaro
7 Los Palos	27 Kelikai	47 Luca	67 Hudo
8 Muapitine	28 Fatumaka/Seical	48 Bubur Liço	68 Mape
9 Ililapa	29 Baucau	49 Dilôr	69 Bobonaro
10 Maluro	30 Berecoli	50 Lacluta (abandoned)	70 Atsabe
11 Leuro	31 Veninale	51 Barike	71 Letefoho
12 Laleno	32 sud Assalaitula	52 Kribas	72 Maliana
13 Tumboro	33 Nahareka and Uaibobo	53 Manatuto	73 Suai
14 Luro	34 Ossu	54 Laclo	74 Ermera
15 Iliomar	35 piste de Meabuti	55 Bettau (Iliamu)	75 Aileu
16 Laivai	36 Beasu	56 Maliana	76 Dili
17 Laga	37 Viqueque	57 Laclubar	77 Turiskai
18 Saelari	38 Bua Nurak	58 Soibada	
19 Atelari	39 Liaruka/Bubuana	59 Mane Hat	
20 Baguia	40 Loilubo/Ostiko	60 Natarbora	

Zones under Indonesian military control

Location of camps along strategic roads

Main roads and tracks

Map 42: Holding camps in East Timor, 1986

From May to September 1981, a new military campaign dubbed the "Fence of Legs" (Pagar Betis) was initiated, a critical error by the Indonesian army. In an attempt to entrap the last resistance groups, all the East Timorese from fifteen to fifty-five years of age were sent from one side of the country to the other and forced to form human chains for Indonesian soldiers to hide behind as they fired on Falintil forces. The operation confirmed to the population that there was nothing to hope for in the occupation forces.

13.3 Revival of the armed resistance

By the end of 1979, with the death or capture of Falintil's main leaders, and the loss of 80 percent of its men and 90 percent of its weapons, the resistance appeared to have been defeated. But in the face of military campaigns, holding camps, and a system of daily oppression, Xanana Gusmão had no difficulty convincing the East Timorese of the need to continue their struggle.

Too limited to conduct a frontal war, Falintil was reorganized into a mobile guerrilla movement. The resistance was divided into two main areas of action. At the center, between the towns of Ermera, Liquica, Aileu, and Dili, ambushes were conducted, such as the attack on the new Indonesian broadcasting antenna in Dili in January 1980. The main forces of resistance were located in

Indonesian soldiers holding the severed heads of Timorese fighters

the eastern part of the territory so its military offensives were concentrated there.

Resistance was only one of Falintil's strategies. Many women remaining in Dili also contributed to the operations, like the young Maria Gorete Joaquim, who stole information from the occupation army before being arrested and tortured in 1979.

The Catholic Church also defended the people. Monsignor Martinho da Costa Lopes did not hesitate to oppose the occupation forces and to publish critical texts before the Indonesian army succeeded in obtaining his resignation in 1983.

In March 1981, the first national conference was organized by the resistance. The fighters endorsed the new strategy and formalized a system of clandestine organization in the camps and in the cities called NUREP (popular resistance groups). This meeting also led to the creation of the first East Timorese platform, the Revolutionary Council of National Resistance (CRRN), which, in 1988, became the CNRM (National Council of Resistance Maubere), and then in 1998, the CNRT (National Council of Timorese Resistance).

Maria Gorete Joaquim   Pope John Paul II and Msgr Martinho da Costa Lopes, 1983

13.4 The negotiations of March 1983 and the continuation of the struggle

Given the failure of violence, in March 1983, Colonel Purwanto, the new Indonesian military commander, proposed holding negotiations. Two meetings were held in the eastern part of the country. However, the positions were irreconcilable. The Indonesian army would only negotiate for the surrender of the guerrillas. The Fretilin delegation, led by Xanana Gusmão, was only ready to accept the principle of an Indonesian "transitional" administration with the deployment of a UN peacekeeping force and the organization of a self-determination referendum. These negotiations allowed the establishment of a ceasefire. The resistance took this opportunity to revive its contacts with dispersed groups and to rethink its organization.

In August 1983 the Indonesian army called off the ceasefire with Operation *Sapu Bersih* ("Total cleanup"). More mobile than in 1977–1978, the guerrillas, who then numbered about sixty-two hundred grouped into ten units, avoided confrontation. The Falintil fighters often escaped the attacks, eventually taking advantage of popular upheavals. The guerillas even managed to reverse the situation at the beginning of the rainy season by attacking several Indonesian convoys. These glorious deeds allowed them to reconstitute their armaments. Discouraged by these setbacks, the Indonesian military command gave up the idea of launching large-scale operations for two years.

At the end of 1985, the resistance increased its activities further. Over a period of ten months, fifty actions were carried out by Falintil. In response, the Indonesian army launched Operation *Kikis* ("Total elimination"). Troops numbering forty thousand were given the mission of capturing Xanana Gusmão. Despite air support and attacks on the Matabean and Kablaki mountains, they failed to do so. For their part, informed by Timorese who had infiltrated into the Indonesian army, Falintil managed to stage several spectacular operations, including the symbolic seizure of Viqueque, which they held for three days in October 1986.

One of the great strengths of the East Timorese resistance was to never use violence against civilians, and especially against the Indonesian transmigrants who were being sent to East Timor as settlers since January 1980.

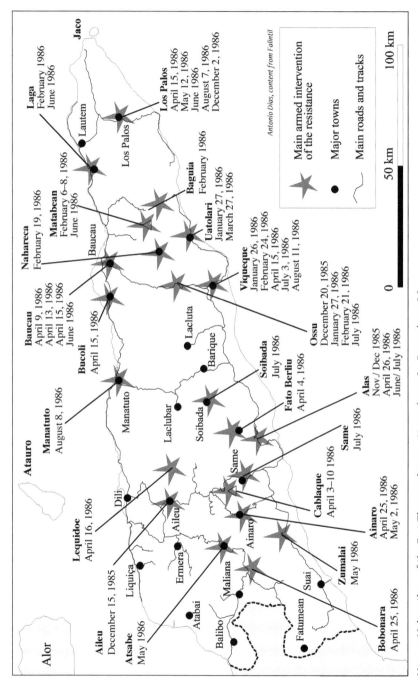

Map 43: Main actions of the East Timor resistance, November 1985–December 1986

In December 1987, General Murdani, one of the key initiators of the invasion, acknowledged to the press that it would take years to overcome a guerrilla force so well established. Yet, at the time, the international community was closing its eyes to what was happening in East Timor.

Mário Carrascalão and Xanana Gusmão, March 1983

Colonel Purwanto and Xanana Gusmão, March 1983

Chapter 14

FROM POPULAR DEMONSTRATIONS TO REFERENDUM, 1989–1999

Overview

In 1989, the partial opening of the territory gave the East Timorese the opportunity to show the world that they were still fighting. Repression aroused reaction from the international community. Two defenders of their people, Bishop Belo and José Ramos Horta, won the Nobel Peace Prize.

The Asian crisis of 1998 brought down the dictatorship of General Suharto and allowed the signing of an agreement on May 5, 1999, which led to the organization of a referendum on self-determination.

14.1 The "opening up" of 1989 and the visit of Pope John Paul II

After fourteen years of total closure, it was difficult to continue prohibiting foreigners from visiting East Timor. It became impossible to justify what the Indonesian army claimed to be a "normalized" situation. In addition, Mário Carrascalão, a founding member of the UDT who had agreed to take the governorship under the Indonesian occupation, made frequent complaints. In August 1989, he did not hesitate to stigmatize the poor living conditions of the population during a session in the Indonesian parliament. In view of the projected visit of Pope John Paul II to Indonesia in 1989, General Suharto was obliged to accept a partial opening up of a few districts, including Dili.

In October 1989, during the pope's visit to Dili, despite a massive police presence, demonstrators deployed nationalist banners before the international press. Forty young people were arrested. Three months later, in January 1990, new demonstrations were strongly suppressed during the visit of John Monjo,

Servizio fotografico de l'O.R.

Servizio fotografico de l'O.R.

Pope John Paul II in Dili, October 1989

the US ambassador to Indonesia. In September 1990, Australian journalist Robert Domm managed to escape the surveillance of the Indonesian army and venture into the mountains for two days, where he managed to interview Xanana Gusmão.

After fifteen years of occupation, this first contact between the resistance and the Western press helped to revive international interest. The Timorese resistance was especially anxious about the visit of a delegation of Portuguese members of parliament, scheduled for November 4–16, 1991. Since 1989, Xanana Gusmão had ordered the resistance not to launch any major new offensives in order to avoid jeopardizing the visit. Realizing that they might somehow lose control of the situation, the Indonesian military set stricter requirements for hosting the delegation. The conditions became so unacceptable that Portugal preferred to suspend the visit.

Xanana Gusmão (*left*) with Ma Huno and Mau Hodu, of Falintil, around 1989

Aitahan Matak (*left*) and Taur Matan Ruak, with villagers, 1991

14.2 The Santa Cruz massacre in 1991 and the capture of Xanana Gusmão

On November 12, 1991, several thousand people gathered for the funeral of a young demonstrator, killed during the visit of Pieter Kooijmans, the UN special rapporteur on torture. The funeral ended in a new demonstration, with many young people brandishing pro-independence banners. The Indonesian army fired into the crowd in the cemetery of Santa Cruz, in front of the camera of journalist Max Stahl. These images, broadcast over Western television networks, led several countries to stop their financial aid to Indonesia. Meanwhile, the United States froze their military assistance. A commission of inquiry appointed by General Suharto announced an official death toll of "about 50 dead." Human rights organizations provided a list of names for the 271 dead, 382 wounded, and 250 missing.

The shooting at Santa Cruz created a spirit of international solidarity. In January 1992 the ferry *Lusitania Expresso* left Portugal with senior politicians and journalists of all backgrounds. However, in March 1992, under threat of the Indonesian navy, it was obliged to stop at the limits of East Timor's territorial waters.

Three photos: Images Max Stahl

Santa Cruz demonstration, November 12, 1991

TEMPO, 4 JANUARI 1992   9

Caricature in the Indonesian magazine *Tempo*: "If there are only fifty dead, where is my grave?"

A few months later, on November 20, 1992, Xanana Gusmão was arrested in Dili. Initially condemned to life imprisonment by an Indonesian military court, his sentence was later commuted to twenty years' imprisonment.

Paradoxically, though the Indonesia army had tried in vain to catch him for more than fifteen years, his capture gave a new impetus to East Timorese nationalism. On the occasion of a meeting of Asia-Pacific countries in Jakarta in November 1994, many East Timorese students did not hesitate to challenge the Indonesian police and army in the capital city, calling for independence and the liberation of their leader. It is no coincidence that, during his official visit to Indonesia in July 1997, South African president Nelson Mandela insisted on obtaining the authorization to meet Xanana Gusmão in prison. The leader had become the symbol of the injustice committed against the East Timorese people.

Many Timorese youths studying in Indonesia had also been imprisoned for conducting pro-independence activities, such as Fernando de Araújo "Lasama," the secretary general of the student network Renetil (Resistência Nacional dos Estudantes Timor-Leste) in 1992.

Young East Timorese putting Indonesian police to flight in Dili, November 14, 1994

Fernando "Lasama" and João Câmara on trial by an Indonesia court, 1994

14.3 The Nobel Peace Prize in 1996 and the creation of the CNRT

In this new context, leaders and representatives of the East Timorese political parties from the mid-1970s who were living among the diaspora met in June 1995 in Austria in order to appease old rivalries and to discuss the future. However, the award of the Nobel Peace Prize in October 1996 to José Ramos Horta, together with the Bishop of Dili, Carlos Filipe Ximenes Belo, seemed to show that the problem could be solved internationally. The bishop had also been able to play a key role, especially since, unlike Xanana Gusmão (in jail in Indonesia since his capture in 1992) or Ramos Horta (in exile), he could more easily interact with the East Timorese resistance, the Indonesian authorities, and UN representatives who were visiting the country. In November 1996 an unprecedented crowd welcomed him upon his arrival. Two hundred thousand people, a quarter of the population, waited for him outside the airport at Dili.

Courtesy Stephane Dovert

Msgr Carlos Filipe Ximenes Belo, 1989

Nobel Peace Prize awarded to East Timorese defenders, 1996

Even if the stakes had moved to the diplomatic field, Falintil maintained its actions, with some fighters dying for liberty, such as David Alex in June 1997, and Konis Santana in March 1998. Others managed to continue the struggle, including Somotxo and Taur Matan Ruak.

The first convention of the National Council of Timorese Resistance (CNRT) in Portugal in April 1998 brought together onto a single platform the five parties of 1975. Representatives of the UDT and Fretilin, but also of Apodeti, Aditla, Kota, and Trabhalista, decided to join forces for a common claim for independence, and chose for president and vice president respectively Xanana Gusmão (still in prison in Jakarta) and José Ramos Horta. Mário Carrascalão was designated as second vice president, but secretly, because he was still living in Timor.

David Alex, 1983

Somotxo and Konis Santana, 1997

Thus, while the international community had maintained a very passive attitude for over twenty years, it was through the ability of the Timorese to resist in the mountains, in the streets, and on the international stage that they won their right to independence.

14.4 The turning point of the Asian crisis of 1998 and the agreement of May 5, 1999

In 1997, the arrival of Kofi Annan at the UN Secretariat brought a new willingness to find a resolution, notably through the appointment of a personal representative of the secretary-general for East Timor, the Pakistani Jamsheed Marker. The same year, the Asian crisis also radically modified the situation. In May 1998, ten months after the beginning of the crisis, the Indonesian economy demonstrated its fragility, weakened as it was by corruption and nepotism. Two-thirds of Indonesia's population fell below the poverty line. Indonesian students openly demonstrated against the dictatorship of General Suharto and occupied the House of Parliament in Jakarta, forcing the old dictator to resign after thirty-three years in power. His vice president, Jusuf Habibie, succeeded him on May 21, 1998.

On June 9, President Habibie proposed a "special status" for East Timor. Six days later, fifteen thousand East Timorese students descended on the streets of Dili demanding a real self-determination referendum and the release of Xanana Gusmão. In the following month, sixty-five thousand Indonesians fled the country. They were mostly transmigrants.

Concurrently, Indonesia resumed negotiations with Portugal. But this was a time of turmoil for East Timor. On August 12, 1998, Indonesian officers brought together anti-independence militia that they had created, asking them to "protect the integration." In a few months, those militias grew from twelve hundred to about nine thousand members.

On November 20, 1998, in a context of rising violence, UN secretary general Kofi Annan expressed his deep concern and Portugal suspended the talks. However, the process was initiated. In January 1999, the Indonesian president declared that he would request the National Assembly (MPR) to approve the choice of independence if his project of "autonomy" (that is, of integration with Indonesia) was rejected.

On May 5, 1999, a tripartite agreement was signed between the United Nations, Portugal, and Indonesia. This agreement scheduled a UN-supervised "popular consultation." The people would have to decide whether or not they wanted the status of "autonomy" within the unitary Republic of Indonesia. Rejection of this proposal by the voters would lead to the "separation of East Timor from Indonesia."

UN Photo/ Eskinder Debede

Signature of the agreement between Portugal and Indonesia on May 5, 1999, under UN supervision

Chapter 15

FROM REFERENDUM TO INDEPENDENCE, 1999–2002

Overview

Despite intimidation and violence, the referendum took place on August 30, 1999. Over 78 percent of the East Timorese population voted for independence.

Militias backed by some Indonesian forces destroyed more than 90 percent of office buildings and forced a third of the East Timorese population into West Timor. At least fourteen hundred people were killed. To end the unrest, an international force was sent to East Timor in September 1999.

From October 1999 to May 2002, the country was placed under UN administration, prior to independence on May 20, 2002.

15.1 The referendum of August 30, 1999, and the arrival of INTERFET

In May–June 1999, UNAMET, the United Nations team in charge of preparing the referendum, ascertained that the militias were intimidating and sometimes murdering Timorese believed to be pro-independence. In July 1999, more than ninety thousand people had to take refuge in the mountains to escape the attacks. To try to end the violence, the high commissioner for human rights, Mary Robinson, proposed sending a UN peacekeeping force. General Wiranto, commander of the Indonesian army, rejected the proposal, leaving the Timorese people exposed to more suffering.

On August 30, 1999, despite the threats and unrest, over 98 percent of East Timorese went to the polls. With such an overwhelming mobilization, the outcome of the election was predictable. On September 1, even before the

Photo Frédéric Durand

Destroyed building in Dili, 1999

Photo Stéphane Dovert

UN "Blue Helmets" in Timor, 2002

announcement of the results, militias supported by some army units began to systematically destroy public buildings. The official results, announced on September 4, 1999, showed that 78.5 percent of the population had voted for independence. The final count precluded any contestation, but the violence did not stop.

In the following days, most government buildings were destroyed while three hundred thousand people were forcibly displaced to West Timor. Hundreds of thousands of East Timorese fled to the mountains to avoid summary executions by the militias or the occupation army.

On September 10, US president Bill Clinton declared that the involvement of the Indonesian army was unacceptable. Two days later, Indonesian president Yusuf Habibie accepted the sending of an international intervention force, INTERFET. Under Australian command, this force arrived in Dili on September 20 and secured the country by the beginning of October 1999.

Photo Frédéric Durand

Ruined building in Dili, 1999

Photo Stéphane Dovert

Destruction of Dili Polytechnic School, 1999

15.2 A tentative appraisal of the death toll

East Timorese people lived through one of the greatest human tragedies of the second half of the twentieth century. There is still no definitive data, but the loss of life was enormous. According to Indonesian sources, the occupation led to at least 150,000 deaths (80,000 related to military operations and 70,000 to the famines of the 1970s). Abílio Osório Soares, who was appointed governor by the Indonesian administration, acknowledged in 1994 the figure of 200,000 deaths since the invasion. In October 2005, the report of the Truth and Reconciliation Commission (CAVR) indicated that the number of victims might reach 183,000. Many independent sources believe that the death toll of the occupation from 1975 to 1999 could be at least 250,000. Solely for the period of the 1999 Referendum, the Joint Commission for Truth and Friendship (CTF) between Indonesia and Timor-Leste concludes that there were 1,400 deaths.

In any case, these figures are shocking if one considers that the total population of East Timor was approximately 700,000 in 1975.

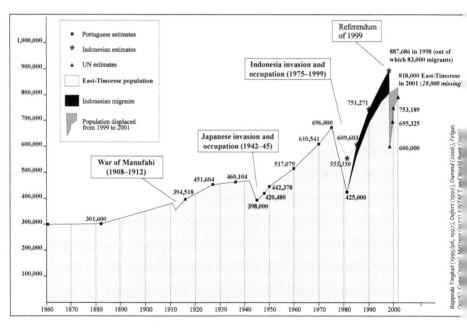

Figure 1: Population of East Timor, 1860-2001

The occupation of East Timor also had dramatic consequences for many young Indonesians who were sent into this war declared under the dictatorial regime of General Suharto. According to internal assessments by the Indonesian army, which are supported by estimates from Falintil, 17,000 Indonesian soldiers may have died in East Timor.

In addition to these very high casualties, trauma caused by the conflict and the occupation were also heavy and difficult to assess.

15.3 The transition to independence under UNTAET, 1999–2002

On October 25, 1999, the UN Security Council established a transitional administration known as UNTAET, managed by the Brazilian Sergio Vieira de Mello. He worked with a National Advisory Council at first headed by Xanana Gusmão, and then, from April 2001, by Manuel Carrascalão.

The country received significant international assistance, with many peacekeepers and foreign experts. Over eight thousand international personnel were working in East Timor in 2000.

Questions to be addressed were many and difficult: the repatriation of the three hundred thousand people forcibly displaced to West Timor in September 1999; the monitoring of the border; the establishment of the Truth and Reconciliation Commission; the renegotiation with Australia of the agreements on resource exploitation in Timor Sea; the election of a constituent assembly; the normalization of diplomatic relations with Indonesia; and reconstruction.

UN Photo/ M. Kobayashi

Displaced East Timorese in Kupang (West Timor) awaiting repatriation, October 1999

On August 30, 2001, elections for a constituent assembly with a mandate to prepare a national constitution were won by Fretilin with 57.4 percent of the vote. This assembly became the country's first parliament.

Kofi Annan, Xanana Gusmão, and Sergio de Mello in Dili, February 2000

First day of school at Fatu Ahi, March 2, 2000

15.4 The presidential elections and the declaration of independence on May 20, 2002

On April 14, 2002, presidential elections were held. Francisco Xavier do Amaral, the first president of the Democratic Republic of Timor-Leste, ran against resistance leader Xanana Gusmão. The two men went together to the same polling station to embody the principles of friendship and reconciliation. Xanana Gusmão was elected with over 82 percent of the vote. He appointed Mari Alkatiri as prime minister.

Independence was officially proclaimed in Dili on May 20, 2002, in the presence of UN secretary-general Kofi Annan and of many other dignitaries, including Jorge Sampaio, president of Portugal, Megawati Sukarnoputri, the Indonesian president, and Bill Clinton, former president of the United States.

People in front of political posters with Xanana Gusmão portraits, 2002

Mari Alkatiri, 2002

Kofi Annan and young Timorese, May 20, 2002

Images Max Stahl

Kofi Annan and Xanana Gusmão in Dili, May 20, 2002

UN Photo/Mark Garten

Speech by Xanana Gusmão to the United Nations, September 27, 2002

The peoples of East Timor, after millennia of evolving as separate kingdoms and decades of opposing colonization and occupation, had finally been able to unite. They had succeeded in gaining the right to build their own nation, and as such, became the first state to join the United Nations in the twenty-first century. The tasks to be accomplished were tremendous, as the country set out to define and carry out its social project, respecting its secular traditions while joining the contemporary world.

The children of the old crocodile still had a long journey ahead of them.

First Timor-Leste government, May 20, 2002

GUERRIERS DE TIMOR.

Timorese warriors

Historical Chronology of Timor-Leste

40,000 BC First traces of people in the eastern part of Timor (Tutuala).

2,500 BC New settlements in the eastern part of the island that could be linked to the first major waves of migrations of Austronesian populations from South China towards Southeast Asia.

300 BC Bronze ring found in eastern Timor suggests relations with the civilizations of the Bronze Age.

c. 1150–1650 Period of construction of stone fortresses (*tranqueiras*).

c. 1250 Timor is identified as an island rich in sandalwood by the head of foreign trade in imperial China.

c. 1350 Timor is listed as an overseas trade destination in Chinese navigation treaties.

1436 A Chinese chronicle describes Timor as a mountainous island covered with sandalwood forests.

1511 The Portuguese seize the Sultanate of Malacca in the Malay Peninsula thereby opening for themselves the route to China and the Spice Islands.

1512 First Portuguese representation of Timor, "the island where sandalwood originates," by the cartographer Francisco Rodrigues.

1514 First known Western written reference to Timor by the Portuguese navigator Rui de Brito in a letter to King Manuel I.

1520 The Portuguese begin trade activities in Cupão (Kupang, West Timor) and in Lifau (Oecussi enclave) where a Topass (mixed race) community develops and serves as an intermediary between the local chieftains and the Europeans.

1522 During his voyage around the world with Magellan, the Italian Pigafetta sojourns in Timor and meets the chieftains of Amaban, Balibo, Suai, and Camenasse.

1556 The Dominicans who form the first religious community of the region estimate 5,000 Catholics in Timor and in the small neighboring islands.

1613 First trade contracts between the Dutch East Indies Company (VOC) and the chieftains of western Timor.

1616 The Dutch temporarily leave the islands of Flores and Timor.

1636 The Dutch drive the Portuguese away from the island of Solor. The latter take refuge in the island of Flores and the westernmost part of Timor at Kupang.

1640 Twenty-two churches are identified in Timor.

1641 The Dominicans convert several Timorese chieftains. The Dutch attack Malacca and drive out the Portuguese.

1642 First Portuguese victory over the kingdom of Wehale. This marks the beginning of the territorial conquest of Timor.

1644 The Dutch attack the port of Cupão/Kupang. They are pushed back.

1645 The Portuguese begin the construction of a fort in the vast Bay of Kupang at the western tip of Timor island.

1651 Capture of Kupang by the Dutch. The Portuguese are constrained to take refuge in Lifau, Oecussi.

1658 The Jesuits found a community in Motael, near Dili.

1661 First treaty between Portugal and VOC. The Dutch acknowledge the sovereignty of the Portuguese over Solor and a major part of the island of Timor, but make them accept the Dutch presence in Kupang.

1673–93 The mixed race community of Topasses, or "Black Portuguese," takes actual control of the Portuguese-speaking territories of Larantuca (Flores), Solor, and Timor.

1702 Arrival of the first Portuguese governor of East Timor, António Coelho Guerreiro.

1705 Governor Coelho Guerreiro has to flee Lifau under pressure from the Topasses.

1719 Camenasse pact. Several Timorese chieftains led by the *liurai* of Cailaco form an alliance against the Portuguese.

1726 Battle of Cailaco between Timorese kingdoms and Portuguese troops.

1738 Establishment of a seminary in Oecussi.

1749 The Topasses, who had raised an army against the Dutch, are routed in the battle of Penfin near Kupang.

1756 The Dutch sign the treaty of Paravicini with fifteen *liurais* of West Timor and extend further their influence in the western part of the island.

1766 Assassination of Portuguese governor Dionisio Gonsalves Rebelo Galvao by the Topasses.

1769 AUG 11 In the face of attacks by the Timorese chieftains and the Dutch menace, the Portuguese governor António Teles de Menezes decides to shift the administrative capital from Lifau to Dili, where a trading post had been functioning since the sixteenth century.

1779–1807 The *reino* of Luca resists the Portuguese colonization during the "War of the Mad."

1796 Construction of a fort in Dili.

1799 Fire in Dili. A major part of the archives is destroyed.

1811 The viceroy of the Indies, Bernardo José Maria de Lorena, writes the "Sarzedas," a document that compiles information about the territory.

1815 First attempts, hardly fruitful, at coffee cultivation in East Timor.

1818 The Dutch settle in Atapupu (twenty kilometers to the west of the Portuguese military post at Batugade on the northern frontier) and in the island of Pantar.

1834 Following the decision of King Pedro IV (May 30) forbidding religious orders in Portugal and its overseas territories, Dominicans are expelled from Timor (until 1854).

1844 Portuguese East Timor becomes a district of the province of Macao, independent of Portuguese India. Dili is declared a free port for international trade.

1850 Timor and the adjacent islands obtain the status of full-fledged provinces. They are no longer dependent on Macao.

1851 In a draft treaty, Governor Lopes de Lima and the Dutch authorities recognize the partition of the island of Timor. In addition, the Dutch offer to concede the *reino* of Maubara if the Portuguese agree to give up the adjacent islands (for example, Flores, Solor, Adonara, Lomblem).

1852 Portugal feels that the concessions accepted by Governor Lopes de Lima concerning subjects not coming under his purview are unacceptable. He is dismissed. Timor and the adjacent islands are once again placed under the administrative supervision of Macao.

1858 Abolition of slavery.

1859 APR 20 A new treaty ratifies the frontiers negotiated in 1851. However, certain ambiguities remain about the exact boundaries. Portuguese Timor is divided into ten military districts.

1860 Governor Affonso de Castro makes an inventory of forty-seven *reinos* dependent on Portugal in the province of Belos and two in the province of Servião (Ambeno and Oecussi).

1863 East Timor gets back its administrative autonomy. Governor Affonso de Castro divides the Portuguese part of Timor into eleven districts (*distritos*), which regroup several *reinos*. Faced with the decline in the production of sandalwood, the governor encourages the development of coffee plantations based on the methods of the Dutch in Java.

1864 Dili is raised to the status of a city (*cidade*).

1866 Following a series of troubles, East Timor once again loses its administrative autonomy (until 1896). Another fire in Dili destroys the last of the archives of Lifau (cf. 1799).

1867–1894 Numerous Portuguese offensives against the Timorese *reinos* who resist the extension of colonial power.

1874 Timor passes from the jurisdiction of the diocese of Goa to that of Macao.

1879 Founding of the first library in Timor (in the Mission of Lahane).

1881–1888 Establishment of a number of facilities and systems, including the lighthouse at the port and the first public schools.

1887 MAR 3 The Portuguese governor Lacerda Maia dies in Dili during a Timorese revolt.

1891 Inauguration of a direct maritime connection between Macao and East Timor.

1893 Signing of a convention between The Hague and Lisbon for marking the boundary between the two parts of Timor.

1884 Illumination of the city of Dili with oil from Laclubar.

1892 Exploration of the hydrocarbon resources of East Timor. No commercially exploitable site is discovered.

1895 First Manufahi War. Most of the *reinos* of the western part of the Portuguese-speaking colony revolt, forcing the Portuguese authorities to mobilize more than twelve thousand men.

1897 Founding of the SAPT, which would become the major colonial enterprise of the island.

1898 Beginning of the physical demarcation of the boundary between the two parts of the island.

1899 Foundation of a seminary at Soibada.

1900 Second Manufahi War.

1902 The Portuguese and the Dutch commence a first series of territorial adjustments, the former, in particular, giving up their claim to the Noimuti enclave.

1904 OCT 1 The Hague convention on the boundary between the two colonies of East and West (Dutch) Timor. Portugal exchanges the territories of Noimuti, Tahakay, and Tamira Ailala for the kingdom of Maukatar.

1906 The Portuguese abolish the former system of tribute (*finta*) paid by the chiefdoms and replace it by a per capita tax.

1909 Portuguese intellectuals denounce the colonial regime in East Timor.

1910–1912 Great Manufahi War against the Portuguese under the command of Dom Boaventura.

1910 In the wake of Portugal becoming a republic, numerous members of religious orders are expelled from East Timor (up to 1924). Most of the schools are closed. Portuguese East Timor is given the status of an overseas province.

1912 Governor Filomeno da Câmara Melo Cabral nationalizes the lands of several chiefdoms and establishes a system of forced agriculture.

1914 Decree of the International Court of Justice fixing the boundary between the two colonies of the island of Timor.

1916 NOV 1 Official exchange of the zones that were the subject of litigations between the Portuguese and the Dutch.

1920 With "pacification," the Portuguese military command regions (fifteen existed in 1908) are progressively transformed into subdistricts (*postos*).

1926 Ban on the cutting of sandalwood to preserve the last natural resources of the island.

1927 Failure of a Portuguese project of installing Timorese people in the "new villages."

1930 António Salazar becomes the minister of colonies and promulgates the Colonies Act.

1934 Beginning of a maritime Japanese link between the Japanese territories of Micronesia (Palau) and Dili.

1936 A Japanese company acquires 40 percent of the shares of the SAPT, the main Portuguese agro-industrial company of East Timor. A Dutch entrepreneur begins the first industrial exploitation of manganese near Baucau.

1939 Inauguration of a weekly flight leaving Darwin for London via East Timor. The Portuguese government authorizes an Australian company to commence a series of petroleum explorations.

1940 SEP 4 Establishment of the diocese of Dili.

1941 Arrival of Australian troops in Dili despite Lisbon's neutrality, to prevent Timor from serving as the entry point for the Japanese invasion of their country.

1942 FEB 19 Japanese invasion of the Portuguese part of the island of Timor.

1945 AUG The Indonesian constituent assembly set up during the Japanese occupation of the Dutch Indies decides not to include East Timor in its territorial claims, limiting it to former colonial frontiers.

1952 Official abolition of the East Timorese chiefdoms.

1952 Visit to East Timor of the Portuguese minister for overseas territories.

1958 MAY 5 President Sukarno visits Lisbon, reaffirming that Indonesia has no intention of annexing East Timor.

1959 JUN 7–20 Viqueque uprising in the context of the presence of fourteen Indonesian refugees; five hundred to one thousand dead.

* First economic development plan for Timor, 1959–1965.

1960 DEC 14 The UN places East Timor on the list of territories to be decolonized.

1963 JUL 9 The Australian parliamentarian Gough Whitlam declares that the right to self-determination of the people of Portuguese Timor ought to be guaranteed by the UN.

1963 NOV 22 By decree no. 45378, East Timor is given the status of a Portuguese overseas province with the same legal status as the other Portuguese provinces.

1967 Creation of two forest reserves in East Timor in the regions of Tilomar and Lore.

1970 JAN A group of young Timorese critical of colonization form an association in Dili. It includes, in particular, Nicolau Lobato, José Ramos Horta, and Mari Alkatiri.

1972 MAY 2 The Portuguese national assembly votes to give a certain autonomy to the overseas territories and plans the creation of local legislative assemblies, elected but placed under the presidency of a governor appointed by Lisbon.

1973 MAR 24 Banning of *Seara*, one of the three newspapers of East Timor. Future political personalities of the territory contributed articles to the paper.

1974

FEB 22 In his book *Portugal and the Future*, General Spinola affirms that the problems of the colonies cannot be resolved by war.

MAR 14 President Caetano relieves Generals Francisco da Costa Gomes and António de Spinola of their command as they are against colonial wars.

APR 14 The church takes a stand against the Caetano government on the question of colonial wars.

APR 25 The MFA (Movement of Armed Forces), initiated by the young officers of the Portuguese army, puts an end to the dictatorial regime of President Caetano in a movement known as the Carnation Revolution.

MAY 11 Founding of the Timor Democratic Union (UDT).

MAY 13 Creation of a commission in Lisbon for the self-determination of East Timor.

MAY 15 General Spinola is proclaimed president of the Republic of Portugal.

MAY 20 Founding of the Social Democratic Association of Timor (ASDT).

1974 (*CONT.*)

MAY 27 Founding of the pro-Indonesian party, Popular and Democratic Association of Timor (Apodeti).

JUN 17 The Indonesian minister for foreign affairs, Adam Malik, writes to ASDT to ensure that Indonesia supports the process of East Timorese independence.

JUL 27 General Spinola, who became the president of Portugal after the Carnation Revolution, recognizes the right to independence of the colonies.

AUG 16 The Indonesian general Ali Murtopo's first visit to Lisbon.

AUG 19 António de Almeida Santos, Portuguese minister for inter-territorial coordination, visits East Timor.

SEP 6 In a meeting with President Suharto, the Australian prime minister Gough Whitlam declares that an independent East Timor would not be a viable state.

SEP 12 The ASDT changes its name and becomes the Revolutionary Front for the Independence of Timor-Leste (Fretilin).

SEP 27 General Spinola resigns and is replaced by General Francisco da Costa Gomes as the president of Portugal.

OCT 14 Second visit to Lisbon by General Ali Murtopo, chief of the Indonesian service of Special Operations (Opsus).

OCT 15 The Portuguese government recognizes India's sovereignty over its former possessions, Goa, Daman, and Diu, annexed by India in 1961.

NOV 18 Arrival of the Portuguese governor, Mário Lemos Pires, in East Timor.

DEC Governor Lemos Pires allots an hour every week on the radio to the different East Timorese political parties to help establish the process of accession to independence.

DEC 4 António de Almeida Santos, Portuguese minister for inter-territorial coordination, declares in the UN that there can only be two solutions for East Timor: maintaining a link with Portugal or integration with Indonesia.

DEC 25 Cyclone Tracy ravages the airport of Darwin. The necessary stopovers in Indonesia complicate the communications between Portugal and East Timor for several months.

1975

JAN Fretilin sets up its first literacy program classes.

- The withdrawal of some Portuguese military troops begins.
- Governor Mário Lemos Pires informs the president of the Portuguese republic by letter about the non-representation of Apodeti and the troubles caused by Indonesia. He suggests sending a UN interim force of fifty to one hundred persons.

1975 (*CONT.*)

JAN Governor Lemos Pires forms the first decolonization commissions.

JAN 5 Founding of the Popular Organization of East Timorese Women (OPMT).

JAN 21 UDT/Fretilin coalition on the program of total independence.

FEB 18 Failure of a simulated landing in East Timor organized by the Indonesian general Murdani in the southern part of the island of Sumatra (Lampung province). The lack of preparation of the Indonesian army makes President Suharto hesitate to launch an invasion.

MAR Partial municipal elections by universal suffrage in the Los Palos region. In July Fretilin wins 55 percent of the seats, a little more than the UDT. Apodeti gets only one seat.

MAR 9 London conference between Portugal and Indonesia.

MAR 11 General Spinola attempts a military coup to regain power in Lisbon.

MAY 27 Under pressure from the Indonesian Information Services (Bakin), the UDT withdraws from its coalition with Fretilin.

JUN 3 First Indonesian military incursion in East Timor (in the Oecussi enclave).

JUN 19 Following the deterioration of the political climate in East Timor, Governor Lemos Pires cancels the radio time allotted to the parties.

JUN 25 A Portuguese delegation meets Indonesian representatives in Hong Kong on the eve of the Macao conference.

JUN 26–28 Macao conference. Fretilin does not participate. Portugal fixes a definite schedule for decolonization, including the election of a constituent assembly in October 1976 and the total transfer of sovereignty two years later.

JUL 5 President Suharto visits the US. President Gerald Ford and Secretary of State Henry Kissinger say they are willing to support the Indonesian stand.

JUL 8 Breakdown of the coalition government in Lisbon ushers in a period of grave political crisis that lasts until November 28, 1975.

JUL 10 The Australian daily *The Age* publishes a declaration by President Suharto stating that the future of East Timor lies in its integration with Indonesia.

JUL 17 Portuguese law on the decolonization of East Timor makes official the schedule finalized in June in Macao that guarantees the independence of the territory.

END OF JUL Several members of the UDT, including João Carrascalão, go to Indonesia. Indonesian officials make it clear to them that they will never accept members of the Fretilin in an East Timorese government.

AUG 6 The UDT delegation returns to Dili.

1975 (*CONT.*)

AUG 8 In Portugal, rupture between President da Costa Gomes and the moderate wing of the Movement of the Armed Forces (MFA). The Portuguese political class is split into three major groups: pro-military regime, pro-popular revolution, and pro-social democracy.

• In Dili, demonstration mar of the UDT representatives towards Fretilin headquarters. The Portuguese police intervenes to avoid confrontation.

AUG 11 Coup by the UDT, commanded by João Carrascalão. A civil war follows for three weeks causing the deaths of between 1,500 and 3,000 persons.

AUG 13 Major João Soares, special envoy of the Portuguese government, is held up for two days at Bali by Indonesian authorities, who prevent him from going to Timor and force him to return to Lisbon.

AUG 14–18 Governor Lemos Pires sends a series of messages to Lisbon asking for instructions but receives no reply whatsoever.

AUG 14 In spite of the non-intervention policy, Colonel Gouveia, chief of police, supports the UDT.

AUG 15 Lino da Silva, the commandant of the military company of Los Palos, joins forces with the UDT.

AUG 18 The garrisons of Maubisse and Aileu join Fretilin. Formation of the Armed Forces for the National Liberation of East Timor (Falintil).

AUG 21 Naval evacuation of most foreigners from the territory.

AUG 24 The Portuguese presidency asks the UN to constitute a goodwill mission comprising Portugal, Indonesia, Australia, and at least one more country of the region.

AUG 26 Governor Lemos Pires takes refuge in the island of Atauro off Dili.

AUG 27 Twenty-three soldiers and three Portuguese civilians authorized earlier to enter West Timor are imprisoned by the Indonesian army.

AUG 28 A Portuguese delegation led by António de Almeida Santos goes to Atauro, then to Jakarta. The Indonesian acting foreign affairs minister, Mochtar Kusumaatmadja, suggests that the delegation sign a memorandum wherein Portugal would ask Indonesia to send a military force for "restoring peace and order."

SEP 1 Fretilin controls de facto the entire territory except for the Oecussi enclave, the island of Atauro, and some UDT pockets on the frontier.

SEP 2 Almeida Santos, on returning to Atauro, drafts an official reply to the Indonesian memorandum project of August. Portugal refuses to allow the Indonesian troops to penetrate East Timorese territory and demands the

1975 (CONT.)

release of the twenty-six Portuguese held in West Timor as a precondition for any future discussion.

SEP 13 After another visit to Jakarta during which he demands in vain the release of the twenty-six Portuguese hostages, António de Almeida Santos returns to Lisbon.

SEP 21 The last of the UDT forces withdraw to West Timor.

SEP 23 The Portuguese governor Lemos Pires attends a meeting on the National Commission on Decolonization held in Lisbon.

SEP 24 A text brought out at the end of the meeting of the National Commission on Decolonization underlines the need "to negotiate with all parties," without mentioning Indonesia.

OCT 8 The first Indonesian attacks on the border city of Batugade. The navy takes part in the operation.

OCT 14 The Indonesian army attacks the city of Maliana. A team of Portuguese journalists is forced to take shelter in the mountains.

OCT 16 Attack on the city of Balibo. During the offensive, the Indonesian army kills five Western journalists.

OCT 24 Rumors about a coup in Lisbon. The armed forces are put on alert.

OCT 31 Governor Lemos Pires goes once again to Portugal for consultation.

NOV 1–2 In Rome, a conference between Portugal and Indonesia resolves to bring together all the parties in Darwin at the end of November.

NOV 18 Indonesian soldiers are captured by Fretilin on East Timorese territory.

NOV 24 Fretilin appeals to the UN requesting an intervention force.

NOV 25 Return of political stability in Portugal.

NOV 27 Indonesia insists that the proposed conference at Darwin be held instead in Bali, leading to its cancellation.

• The Indonesian army seizes the city of Atabae, thereby opening for itself the road to Dili.

NOV 28 Fretilin unilaterally declares independence. Francisco Xavier do Amaral, the president of the party, becomes the first president of the Democratic Republic of East Timor.

NOV 30 The Indonesian authorities get the UDT and Apodeti leaders, who had taken shelter in West Timor, to sign the Balibo declaration demanding the integration of East Timor with Indonesia.

DEC 2 The Indonesian authorities declare to the International Red Cross Committee that they do not recognize its neutrality, causing its delegates to leave the territory.

1975 *(CONT.)*

DEC 4 Five members of the government designated by Fretilin—Mari Alkatiri, Abílio Araújo, Rogério Lobato, José Ramos Horta, and Roque Rodrigues leave Timor to seek foreign support.

DEC 5–6 President Gerald Ford and Secretary of State Henry Kissinger visit Jakarta.

DEC 7 The Indonesian army invades East Timor.

  • Lisbon denounces the Indonesian invasion and breaks off diplomatic ties with Jakarta.

DEC 8 The last of the colonial Portuguese administrators leave the island of Atauro on board the *Afonso Cerqueira*.

DEC 10 The Indonesian army attacks Baucau.

DEC 12 Resolution 3485 of the UN General Assembly asking the Indonesian government "to stop violating the territorial integrity of Portuguese Timor and to withdraw its armed forces immediately from the territory."

DEC 16 Indonesia annexes the Oecussi enclave.

DEC 22 The UN Security Council demands the immediate withdrawal of the Indonesian troops "to enable the East Timorese to freely exercise their right to self-determination."

DEC 25 Second series of Indonesian offensives against Liquiça, Suai, and later in the interior of the territory. Indonesian forces are estimated to be 25,000 strong.

1976

JAN 13 Formation of a "provisional government" by Indonesia.

JAN 18–19 Winspeare Guiccardi, the special envoy of the UN secretary-general, visits East Timor, specifically the Oecussi enclave, the island of Atauro, and the three cities of Dili, Manatuto, and Baucau. In his report submitted to the secretary-general on April 22, he states that he could not meet the representatives of the resistance due to lack of cooperation from Indonesia and Australia.

FEB 13 Francisco Xavier Lopes da Cruz, ex-president of the UDT and the first governor of the Indonesian administration in East Timor, estimates that 60,000 persons have died since the beginning of the turmoil.

MAR 31 The Portuguese parliament adds an article to the National Constitution (no. 389) stipulating Portugal's obligation to guarantee East Timor's right to independence.

APR 3 The members of the UDT rise up against the Indonesian occupation army.

APR 22 Second resolution of the UN Security Council demanding the withdrawal of the Indonesian troops.

1976 (*CONT.*)

APR 25 Governor Lemos Pires is officially relieved of his post as governor of East Timor.

MAY 20 Fretilin holds a two-week national conference at Soibada in the center of the territory (until June 2) to organize the resistance movement.

MAY 31 Presentation of an "Integration Act" by the Indonesian government. The UN refuses to admit this as an internationally acceptable procedure.

JUL 13 Da Costa Gomes abandons the presidency of Portugal. He is replaced by General António Ramalho Eanes.

JUL 17 General Suharto proclaims the integration of East Timor with the Republic of Indonesia as its twenty-seventh province.

JUL 27 A commission is set up in Portugal to shed light on the process of decolonizing Timor (CAEPDT).

JUL 28 Arrival in Lisbon of twenty-three Portuguese army personnel held as hostages by the Indonesian army since August 1975.

SEP 3 The conference of Australian Catholic Bishops expresses the wish to send humanitarian aid to East Timor. No international aid is authorized by the Indonesian army before October 1979.

SEP 29 The Australian government confiscates a radio transmitter that until then had helped the Timorese activists in Darwin communicate with the resistance.

NOV Hidden documents in East Timor show that 20,000 of the 30,000 inhabitants of Dili had applied for emigration to Portugal.

NOV 19 In an internal report, Indonesian observers declare that the death toll since the invasion could rise to 100,000 persons.

 • The UN General Assembly, for the first time, asks for the organization of a referendum for self-determination.

1977

JAN 20 The Australian government recognizes the de facto Indonesian occupation of East Timor.

MAR 13 A hearing on East Timor is held in the American Congress. James Dunn, former Australian consul in Dili, presents his first conclusions on the magnitude of human tragedy.

MAY Nomination of Msgr. Martinho da Costa Lopez, vicar of Dili since 1975, as the apostolic administrator with the powers of a resident bishop.

AUG 17 Beginning of the Indonesian military "encirclement and annihilation" campaign (until March 1979).

SEP 7 Dismissal of Francisco Xavier do Amaral by Fretilin.

1977 (*CONT.*)

OCT 16 Nicolau Lobato is elected president of Fretilin.

NOV 28 The UN General Assembly asks for the organization of a referendum for self-determination for the second time.

1978

JAN 20 Andrew Peacock, minister for foreign affairs in the Australian Liberal government, confirms the stand of the previous government, declaring that "it would be unrealistic to continue refusing to recognize de facto that East Timor is a part of Indonesia."

MAR–JUN Indonesia buys a large quantity of military equipment, especially aircraft: twelve Bell Sioux helicopters suited to guerrilla warfare and six Nomad Searchmaster aircraft from Australia, eight Hawk fighters from the UK, and sixteen A4-Skyhawks from the US.

MAY 12 First records of forced sterilizations in East Timor.

JUL 18 Brief visit of President Suharto to East Timor (Dili and Maliana).

AUG 30 The Indonesian army captures Francisco Xavier do Amaral, former president of Fretilin.

SEP 7–9 Visits to East Timor organized for the benefit of journalists and foreign ambassadors. They express their shock at the extent of famine and mortality in the round-up camps.

NOV 20 The UN General Assembly demands the organization of a referendum of self-determination for the third time.

NOV 22 Fall of the last pocket of East Timorese resistance on Mount Matabean.

DEC 12 The surrender of the radio operator Alarico Fernandes cuts off Fretilin from the rest of the world.

DEC 15 The Labor government in Australia recognizes de jure the annexation of East Timor.

DEC 31 The Indonesian army kills Nicolau Lobato, president of Fretilin and chief of resistance.

1979

JAN Decision of the Indonesian military command to transfer all Portuguese lands to the Indonesian army (Laksuda no. 4/1979).

APR 2 International Red Cross reports indicate that tens of thousands of Timorese are in danger of dying of hunger unless an aid program is quickly organized.

OCT 19 General Suharto authorizes the International Red Cross to set up an aid program restricted to 60,000 beneficiaries. Foreign delegates reveal a health and food supply condition "as bad as that of Biafra and potentially as serious as that of Kampuchea."

1979 (*CONT.*)

NOV 12 During a visit to London with President Suharto, Mochtar Kusumaatmadja, the Indonesian minister for foreign affairs, declares that 120,000 persons have died in East Timor since 1975.

NOV 26 After functioning for four years, the operation Seroja Command, formed for the invasion of East Timor, is disbanded by the Indonesian army as it thinks that it has overcome the resistance.

DEC 13 The UN General Assembly demands the organization of a referendum of self-determination for the fourth time.

DEC 25 The *Times* publishes information about the use of napalm by the Indonesian army in East Timor.

1980

JAN 16 The Indonesian transmigration programs designate East Timor as a destination in programs for the displaced populations migrating from the densely populated islands of Java and Bali to other regions of the archipelago.

FEB 6 The American Congress reproaches the US ambassador to Jakarta for not communicating information about the magnitude of the famine in East Timor.

JUN 10–11 An attack on Dili by Fretilin damages the new broadcasting station set up by the Indonesian authorities.

NOV 11 The UN General Assembly demands the organization of a referendum for self-determination for the fifth time.

1981

MAR 1–8 The resistance, now led by Xanana Gusmão, organizes a conference for the reorganization of the country and constitution of the Revolutionary Council of National Resistance (CRRN).

APR 15 In spite of a new wave of famine, the Indonesian administration prevents the International Red Cross from continuing its activities in East Timor.

JUN 3 In a report meant for President Suharto, the members of the provincial parliament established by the Indonesian authorities complain of extortions committed by the army as well as monopolization of sectors of the economy. Two of the signatories would be arrested on October 18.

JUL 20 Amnesty International expresses its concern after the revelation of military instruction manuals stolen from East Timor that suggest torture as a means for obtaining information during interrogations.

JUL 31 The Timorese clergy publishes "Reflection on Faith," which discusses the humiliation and the suffering of the population.

AUG 19 Beginning of the operation Pagar Betis, or "Fence-of-legs."

1981 (*CONT.*)

SEP Four hundred to five hundred East Timorese are killed by the Indonesian army at St. Antony, near Lacluta, where the troops fired on dwellings at night with automatic weapons, only to realize the next day that there were only women and children there.

OCT After the ban on using Portuguese by the Indonesian administration, the Vatican approves the decision of the East Timorese clergy to use Tetum, the vernacular of the eastern part of the island, rather than Indonesian during services.

• Australia signs a provisional agreement on fishing with Indonesia covering East Timorese waters (PFSEL, Provisional Fisheries Surveillance and Enforcement Line).

OCT 24 The UN General Assembly demands the organization of a referendum for self-determination for the sixth time.

OCT 26 The Australian parliament decides to conduct an inquiry on the situation in East Timor.

1982

JAN 11 Australian press publishes an appeal by the East Timorese clergy revealing that half the population is threatened with famine.

APR 14 After an interruption of one year, the International Red Cross obtains authorization to work once again in East Timor.

MAY 4 During the first elections organized by Indonesia in East Timor as a part of the national parliamentary elections, General Suharto's Golkar Party obtains 99.43 percent of the votes, which hardly convinces the international community.

MAY 16 Pope John Paul II refuses to include the Diocese of Dili in the conference of Indonesian bishops.

MAY 18–28 Visit of a group of Western journalists highlights the magnitude of the problems of undernourishment in East Timor.

JUN 10 The Portuguese president António dos Santos Ranalho Eanes makes the East Timorese cause one of his priorities.

OCT 13 Msgr. da Costa Lopes, the apostolic administrator of Dili, denounces the massacre of Lacluta (September 1981) in a sermon, incurring the wrath of the Indonesian army.

NOV 3 The UN General Assembly demands the organization of a referendum for self-determination in East Timor for the seventh time.

1983

FEB 7–12 Portuguese journalist Rui Araujo visits East Timor with the permission of the Indonesian government. Despite the tour being prepared by the army, his photographs show the pathetic situation in which the Timorese live.

FEB 16 The UN Human Rights Commission condemns the violence in Timor and demands the implementation of the process of self-determination.

MAR 21–23 Negotiations between the occupying Indonesian army (Col. Purwanto) and the East Timorese resistance (Xanana Gusmão) bring the declaration of a ceasefire.

MAY 13 A document signed by a group of Timorese priests indicates that "the implacable extermination of the Timorese people can be expected."

MAY 16 Indonesia obtains from the Vatican the resignation of the apostolic administrator, Msgr. Martinho da Costa Lopes. His successor, Msgr. Carlos Felipe Belo, a Timorese who had agreed to adopt Indonesian nationality, is poorly received at first. He would reveal himself to be a fervent defender of the rights of the Timorese and would win the Nobel Peace Prize in 1996.

MAY 23 A report by the Center for Defense Information in the US estimates 250,000 deaths in East Timor since the Indonesian invasion in 1975.

JUL 29 A total of 170 European parliamentarians launch an appeal for the right of the East Timorese people to self-determination.

JUL 30 Visit of a delegation of Australian parliamentarians, led by Bill Morrison, in the context of the ceasefire established in March 1983. This visit gives a favorable report on the Indonesian administration.

AUG 17 The Indonesian army calls off the ceasefire. General Benny Murdani, commander in chief of the Indonesian armed forces, declares that the Timorese resistance would be crushed "mercilessly."

AUG 21 Execution of nearly a thousand civilians in the village of Kraras (subdistrict of Ossu near Viqueque).

SEP 9 The Indonesian government decrees a state of emergency in East Timor.

SEP 14 President Suharto demands the launching of a new military operation, Operasi Persatuan, or "Operation Unity."

SEP 23 Even though Indonesia has been occupying East Timor for eight years, the UN General Assembly defers its vote for the year 1983 and asks the secretary-general to ensure the dossier is followed up.

OCT 13 Msgr. Belo preaches against the arrests and violence and declares that Indonesia ought to bring books and food to East Timor rather than arms.

1983 (*CONT.*)

NOV 13 The Indonesian Episcopal Conference (MAWI), previously very reserved, declares its support for the Timorese people, "victims of cruel sufferings." This step shows a spilt from the stand of the papal nuncio of Jakarta, Msgr. Pablo Puente.

DEC 25 The East Timorese clergy refuses to meet General Murdani (of Catholic faith) on Christmas day to protest against the proposed launching of a new military offensive on Jan 2, 1984.

1984

JAN Serious food shortages caused by the military campaigns launched since 1983.

JAN 29 The Angolan minister for information holds a press conference on the situation in East Timor concurrent with a meeting held by the Organization of Non-Aligned countries in Jakarta. General Suharto does not allow Indonesian journalists to attend.

FEB 21 The UN Human Rights Commission grants an audience to Msgr. Martinho da Costa Lopes, former apostolic administrator of Dili, and denounces the actions of Indonesia.

MAR 16 The International Red Cross is authorized to visit the prisoners in Dili but not to bring them humanitarian aid.

MAR 20 The "governor," Mário Carrascalão, admits that there are still at least 2,000 political prisoners on the island of Atauro off the coast of Dili but that they will not be released as long as "the situation is not calm."

MAR 25 Fretilin proposes a peace plan.

MAY 2 Msgr. Belo sends a letter to his predecessor in exile in Portugal indicating that disappearance of people, arrests, and military operations continue and that in spite of the presence of thousands of soldiers the Indonesian army is not in a position to win the war.

JUL 21 The Portuguese president, António dos Santos Ramalho Eanes, and the prime minister, Mário Soares, make a common declaration reminding the Portuguese government of its duty to "guarantee the inalienable right of the East Timorese people to self-determination."

DEC 17 The commander in chief of the Indonesian armed forces, General Benny Murdani, acknowledges that the East Timorese conflict "will take time to be resolved."

1985

JAN 1 The Council of Catholic Priests of East Timor publishes a new declaration on faith revealing the regular use of children as human shields and mass arrests of civilians by the Indonesian army. The East Timorese clergy specially demands that the right to self-determination be respected.

JAN 5 The Indonesian government announces the introduction of a major family planning program concerning 95,000 East Timorese women, that is, more than 60 percent of all women of childbearing age. The World Bank finances the program.

MAR 15 Under pressure from Indonesia, the UN Human Rights Commission withdraws the topic of Timor from its agenda.

MAY 8 One hundred thirty-one members of the American Congress address a letter to President Reagan before his visit to Portugal, expressing their concern over the situation in East Timor.

AUG 18 During a trip to Jakarta, the Australian Labor prime minister Robert Hawke reaffirms that his country recognizes the sovereignty of Indonesia over East Timor. Mr. Hawke had supported Timor's right to self-determination when he was in the opposition.

SEP 14 Reports indicate heavy bombing by the Indonesian air force in the eastern part of the territory. Begun in August 1983, these attacks would continue until June 1984.

SEP 24 Indonesia and Portugal resume diplomatic ties.

OCT 27 Beginning of negotiations between Australia and Indonesia over the sharing of petroleum resources in the Timor Sea.

1986

MAR 31 Formation of a new UDT/Fretilin coalition in Lisbon.

APR 17 Seventy Japanese parliamentarians send a letter to the UN secretary-general demanding the establishment of a process for self-determination in East Timor.

JUL 10 The European parliament votes on a motion affirming the right of the East Timorese people to self-determination.

OCT 20 Four East Timorese students attempt to take refuge in the Netherlands embassy in Jakarta.

NOV Fretilin reveals a new offensive involving more than fifty battalions (nearly 25,000 men) in the eastern part of the territory.

1987

JAN 2 Nomination of General Mantiri as the new Indonesian commandant for military operations in East Timor.

APR 13 The American Episcopal Conference denounces the Indonesian occupation and particularly the forced birth control campaigns.

JUN 5 Forty members of the American senate criticize the Indonesian occupation of East Timor in an open letter to the press.

JUL 14 General Mantiri is relieved of his duties and replaced by Colonel Sonato.

NOV 14 The Indonesian daily *Jakarta Post* reveals a new famine in the south of the country and indicates that 38,000 children are suffering from malnutrition.

DEC Msgr. Belo, the apostolic administrator of Dili, writes a letter accusing the Indonesian army of regularly practicing torture.

1988

FEB 18 The Indonesian government invites the Portuguese parliament to send a delegation.

MAY 3 The governments of the twelve countries of the European Community adopt a common resolution calling upon the UN secretary-general to work towards safeguarding the rights of the East Timorese people.

JUN The Vatican names Msgr. Belo as the bishop of Dili (officially through the offices of the Diocese of Lorium in Italy).

JUN 20 Mário Carrascalão, the governor appointed by Indonesia, asks President Suharto to open territory closed by the army for more than twelve years.

SEP 15 The European parliament asks for the withdrawal of the Indonesian troops and the enforcing of the right of the East Timorese to self-determination.

OCT 30 Two hundred twenty-nine American parliamentarians express their concern over the use of torture and arbitrary imprisonments in East Timor.

NOV 2–3 President Suharto's visit to East Timor and announcement of a "partial opening up" of the territory.

DEC 31 Attack by Fretilin in the suburbs of Dili, causing the death of eighty-four Indonesian soldiers.

1989

JAN 1 Eight of the thirteen districts of East Timor are declared "open" to foreigners by President Suharto. However, more than half of the territory remains under the exclusive control of the Indonesian army.

FEB 6 Bishop Belo of Dili writes to the UN secretary-general demanding the organization of a referendum for self-determination.

1989 (*CONT.*)

APR 26 During a meeting with General Suharto, the American vice president Dan Quayle broaches the question of Indonesia's "repressive practices" in East Timor.

JUN First assassination bid on Bishop Belo. Others would take place in October 1991, December 1996, and September 1999.

JUN 9 One hundred eighteen members of the American Congress write to President George Bush, asking him to take up the East Timor problem during President Suharto's visit to the US.

AUG 5 Mário Carrascalão presents a report before the Indonesian assembly, declaring in particular that the illiteracy rate has reached 92 percent and that more than a third of the subdistricts do not have a single doctor.

AUG 25 The UN Sub-Commission on Prevention of Discrimination and Protection of Minorities advises the Human Rights Commission to continue its supervision of the situation in East Timor.

OCT 5 Xanana Gusmão presents a peace plan foreseeing independence after a period of administrative supervision under the control of Indonesia and then of the UN.

OCT 12 Pope John Paul II's visit to Dili. The demonstrations result in the arrest of forty people.

DEC 11 Indonesia and Australia sign a "provisional agreement of cooperation" for jointly exploiting the hydrocarbon resources in the Timor Sea.

DEC 17 One hundred members of the American Congress ask the State Department to carry out an inquiry into the torture of the people arrested after the visit of Pope John Paul II.

1990

JAN 1 Certain traditional celebrations, including funerals, are banned in the district of Ermera for the reason that they are too extravagant.

JAN 17 Demonstrations are severely repressed on the visit to Dili of John Monjo, the American ambassador to Indonesia.

FEB 3 General Murdani, on a visit to East Timor, threatens severe reprisals if new demonstrations are organized.

MAR New Indonesian military offensive with 40,000 soldiers.

APR 19 Cancellation of a colloquium in Yogyakarta, Java, during which a team of researchers from the University of Gadjah Mada were to present the East Timorese situation.

AUG 17 School children brandish the Fretilin flag in Dili during the Indonesian national festival. They are arrested.

1990 (*CONT.*)

SEP 4 Protest demonstration at the fiftieth anniversary of the creation of the diocese of Dili.

SEP 27 The Australian journalist Robert Domm manages to interview Xanana Gusmão in the neighborhood of Ainaro. This first contact with the foreign press after fifteen years of military occupation reopens the debate on the Timorese problem and incites pro-independence demonstrations in Dili.

OCT Appearance of "ninjas" in Dili. These masked paramilitary groups that carry out nocturnal attacks against separatists are reminiscent of the death squadrons deployed in Java in 1982–83. President Suharto, in his biography, admitted to having authorized their creation.

OCT 15 The police fire on the students of the San Paulus Grammar School in Dili. Three die, three are wounded, and around forty are arrested.

1991

FEB 9 Indonesia and Australia sign a joint treaty of exploitation of oil resources in the Timor Sea confirming the provisional agreement of December 1989.

FEB 22 Portugal lodges a complaint against Australia at the International Court of Justice (ICJ) at The Hague for having signed a treaty with Indonesia on East Timor (Portugal could not summon Indonesia, which does not recognize ICJ).

FEB 27 Death of Msgr. Martinho da Costa Lopes, former apostolic administrator of Dili, in exile in Portugal since 1983.

MAR 11–12 During a visit to Jakarta, the Japanese deputy minister for foreign affairs takes up the question of human rights in East Timor.

MAR 13 Amnesty International denounces the arrest of six East Timorese students in Bali.

JUN 1 Indonesia promulgates a decree prohibiting "foreigners" from owning land in East Timor in order to force the natives to give up their Portuguese nationality. They are given until May 31, 1992, to become Indonesians or have their land expropriated.

JUN 28 The Parliamentary Assembly of the European Council asks the Indonesian government to withdraw its troops from East Timor as a precondition for the process of self-determination. It asks the member states to stop the sale of military equipment to Indonesia.

SEP 13 An agreement signed between Portugal and Indonesia paves the way for the visit of a delegation of Portuguese parliamentarians to East Timor.

OCT 25 The Portuguese parliament suspends its proposed visit to Timor (November 4–16) due to numerous conditions imposed by Indonesia.

1991 (*CONT.*)

NOV 12 The Indonesian army opens fire on a crowd of about 3,500 persons in the neighborhood of the cemetery of Santa Cruz at Dili. Video pictures taken by journalist Max Stahl, telecast over Western channels, results in the suspension of financial aid by several countries (Canada, Denmark, Netherlands). American military aid is also stopped. The first official Indonesian assessment is nineteen deaths and ninety-one injured, whereas the Timorese claim more than two hundred deaths and the disappearance of many people.

NOV 19 In protest against the shooting at Santa Cruz, seventy East Timorese students demonstrate in Jakarta. They are arrested.

NOV 23 A council of students from ten Indonesian universities asks the government to withdraw its troops from East Timor and to allow East Timorese people to exercise their right to self determination.

NOV 28 In response to the pressures of the international community, President Suharto appoints a national inquiry commission, which goes to Dili at the end of November. The new official estimate figuring in its report submitted on December 26, 1991, indicates "about fifty deaths," but except for eighteen tombs, the bodies remain untraceable. Amnesty International, for its part, furnishes a list of names for the 271 dead, 382 wounded, and 250 disappeared.

DEC 19 Arrest of East Timorese students who came to present petitions to several diplomatic chancelleries in Jakarta (UN, Australia, and Japan) protesting the action of the Indonesian army in the territory.

1992

JAN 22 The ferry Lusitania Expresso, baptized the "Ship of Peace," leaves Lisbon for East Timor to "lay floral tributes on the tombs of those killed in Santa Cruz."

JAN 27 Capture of Mau Hudo, the number 2 Fretilin man.

JAN 28 Pieter Kooijmans, special reporter of the UN on torture, points out that the practice of torture by the Indonesian police might be routine in certain regions including East Timor.

FEB Detention for questioning of American, Japanese, and Moroccan travelers who had arrived in East Timor on tourist visas and were suspected to be journalists. They were expelled from the territory on February 27.

MAR 11 The ferry *Lusitania Expresso*, which left Portugal one and a half months earlier, approaches East Timorese territorial waters carrying 120 persons of twenty-one nationalities on board, with the former Portuguese president, General Ramalho Eanes, amongst them. The Indonesian navy forces it to turn back.

1992 *(CONT.)*

MAR 12 Beginning of the trial in Dili of the East Timorese students who demonstrated against the Santa Cruz massacres. They are convicted, with sentences ranging from six years to life imprisonment. On May 29, a court-martial tries two Indonesian soldiers and eight non-commissioned officers for "indiscipline" during the Santa Cruz shooting. The sentences pronounced would not exceed eighteen months' imprisonment.

MAR 14 The new military commandant of East Timor, General Theo Syafei, declares that "if the events such as the ones at Santa Cruz were to happen again, the number of victims would certainly be higher."

• Socialist International appeals for the "withdrawal of Indonesian troops from East Timor."

MAR 25 Dissolution of the IGGI, the inter-governmental group of sponsors for Indonesia, following international reaction provoked by the shooting in Santa Cruz in November 1991.

MAR 30 Closure of the only educational establishment still using Portuguese as the medium of instruction.

APR 10 The World Bank agrees to form a new group of sponsors for Indonesia the CGI (Advisory Group on Indonesia), which meets in Paris.

MAY 2 Two Indonesian lawyers appointed to defend the East Timorese political prisoners challenge the legality of the procedure, arguing that the criminal code of the archipelago (KUHP) is not applicable to their clients as East Timor was not legally integrated with Indonesia. Moreover, they underline the fact that the Indonesian constitution "guarantees all nations the right to liberty."

JUN 25 The American Congress withdraws from the federal budget 2 million dollars of military aid meant for Indonesia.

JUL 4 In an interview with the *Indonesian Weekly* editor, General Mantiri defines the reaction of the army men who fired on the crowd at Santa Cruz as "appropriate."

JUL 16 In the United Kingdom, the House of Lords demands the enforcement of an embargo on the sale of arms to Indonesia, the suspension of economic aid, and the suspension of training programs for Indonesian officers.

JUL 20 Portugal blocks the signature of an agreement between the European Community and ASEAN, citing the violation of human rights in East Timor.

JUL 27 Session of the UN Committee of Decolonization dedicated to East Timor.

AUG 27 The UN Sub-Commission on Prevention of Discrimination and Protection of Minorities "deplores the tragic events of November 12, 1991," "expresses

1992 (*CONT.*)

its concern over continuing violation of human rights in East Timor," and asks Indonesia to immediately provide information about the missing persons.

SEP Mário Carrascalão resigns from his post as governor of East Timor. He is replaced by Abílio Osório Soares, former secretary-general of Apodeti.

NOV 20 Capture of Xanana Gusmão by the Indonesian army.

DEC 11 The Indonesian army forces the members supposed to be part of the resistance to swear loyalty to the Indonesian flag, after consuming a drink that contained their own blood, cock's blood, and whisky. Following a complaint by Bishop Belo, the military commandant, Theo Syafei, forbids this practice.

DEC 17 Meeting in New York of the Portuguese and Indonesian ministers for foreign affairs under the aegis of the UN. The exact contents of the discussions are not divulged.

1993

- Taur Matan Ruak takes over the command of Falintil in the territory.

FEB–MAY Trial of Xanana Gusmão organized by the Indonesian judiciary in Dili. The judges refuse to listen to his plea and sentence him to solitary life imprisonment on May 21. The International Commission of Jurists present during a part of the sessions declared in its report that this trial "did not take place according to international rules and had even violated the provisions of the Indonesian Penal Code."

MAR 10 The UN Human Rights Commission expresses its concern about the activities of Indonesia in East Timor and asks Jakarta to invite special reporters to examine the situation in the territory. The motion had won the support (Australia, Canada, France, US, etc.) or abstention (Japan, Libya, Pakistan, Tunisia, etc.) of several countries that until then had been in favor of Indonesia.

APR 3 The Indonesian army captures Ma'Huno, second in command of the East Timorese resistance.

APR 21 Talks between Portugal and Indonesia under the aegis of the UN in Rome.

JUN 22 The International Red Cross Committee deplores the "continuing difficulties" caused by the Indonesian administration resulting in obstructing visits to East Timorese prisoners.

JUL General Suharto commutes the prison sentence of Xanana Gusmão to twenty years' solitary confinement.

AUG 11 Xanana Gusmão is transferred from Dili to the Kedungpane prison of common law in Semarang (Central Java). He goes on a hunger strike in order to be shifted to the Cipinang detention center for political prisoners in Jakarta.

1993 (*CONT.*)

SEP 17 Negotiations in New York between the Portuguese and Indonesian ministers for foreign affairs, Durao Barroso and Ali Alatas.

NOV 4 The Norwegian Thorolf Rafto Human Rights prize is awarded to the East Timorese people.

DEC 14–17 Beginning of informal negotiations between the pro-Indonesian and anti-Indonesian East Timorese. Abílio Araújo, who leads the delegation of East Timorese resistance, loses his seat for not having followed the instructions given to him.

DEC 30 Seven East Timorese students who had taken refuge in the European embassies in Jakarta obtain authorization to go to Portugal.

1994

FEB The American State Department places Indonesia on its blacklist of countries that do not respect human rights, along with Burma, China, North Korea, and Zaire.

APR 15 Abílio Osório Soares, appointed governor of East Timor in 1992 to replace Mário Carrascalão, admits before foreign journalists to the figure of 200,000 East Timorese deaths since 1975.

MAY 31–JUN 4 Meeting of the Asia-Pacific Coalition for East Timor in Manila. Under pressure from President Suharto, Philippines declares many persons non grata, including Danielle Mitterand, the president of France-Liberté, and the Irish Nobel Peace Prize laureate Maired Maguire.

JUL 14 Five hundred demonstrators gather before the provincial parliament of Dili to demand that freedom of religion be respected. A few days earlier, Indonesian soldiers had trampled on the host during a mass in Remexico, and nuns in Dili had been attacked. The intervention of two anti-riot units against the demonstrators resulted in four deaths and some twenty injured.

JUL 31 Bishop Belo denounces in an open letter "the excessive controls, executions, torture, arrests, and arbitrary detentions, particularly by extra-judiciary institutions."

SEP 15 The Indonesian foreign affairs minister Ali Alatas, who had declared that East Timor was "a pebble in Indonesia's shoes," mentions before the parliament the possibility of granting special status to the territory.

OCT 8 First meeting between Ali Alatas and José Ramos Horta, the CNRT representative. The latter proposes a ceasefire.

OCT 13 Indonesia officially refuses the ceasefire offer of the East Timorese resistance.

1994 (*CONT.*)

OCT 27 The Federal Court of Boston orders the Indonesian general Sintong Panjaitan to pay 14 million dollars to the mother of the young New Zealander Kamal Bamadhaj, killed during the shooting at Santa Cruz in November 1991.

NOV 12 East Timorese demonstration on the occasion of an APEC meeting in Indonesia. Twenty-nine East Timorese students take refuge in the US embassy in Jakarta. Eighty others are "reported missing."

NOV 12–14 Nearly a thousand young Timorese challenge the police in Dili.

1995

JAN 1 During a demonstration in Baucau the army kills three Timorese.

JAN 13 The special UN reporter on extrajudiciary executions submits his report on the 1991 events of Santa Cruz. He concludes that the shooting of November 12 was "the consequence of a planned military operation against unarmed civilians demonstrating their political disagreement."

JUN 2–5 First round of negotiations among the different members of the East Timorese diaspora at Burg Schlaining (Austria).

JUN 30 The International Court of Justice declares its inability to take up the case brought by Portugal against Australia in February 1991 regarding the agreement with Indonesia on oil resources in the Timor Sea.

JUL 9 Negotiations between the Portuguese and Indonesian foreign affairs ministers in Geneva under the aegis of the United Nations.

JUL The army opens fire on the population of the village of Gariana (near Liquiça). At least six persons are killed. Information broadcast outside the country about the troubles that ensued forces the Indonesian army to court-martial two officers. They are sentenced to four years in prison.

AUG 10–18 Visit of a delegation of European parliamentarians to Indonesia. They also get permission to visit East Timor.

SEP 1 The Indonesian army opens fire on the people of a hamlet near Baucau, resulting in three deaths.

SEP/OCT Confrontations between East Timorese and the migrants, particularly in Dili and Maliana, leading notably to the destruction of seven mosques and two protestant churches.

OCT 26 The Indonesian minister for religions, Tarmizi Taher, asks the pope for the creation of a second diocese in East Timor, hoping for the nomination of an Indonesian bishop.

DEC 4 José Ayala Lasso, the high commissioner for human rights, visits East Timor.

DEC 18 Australia and Indonesia sign a defense agreement.

1996

EARLY JAN In a report on the East Timor situation, Amnesty International indicates that at least thirteen summary executions of civilians took place in 1995 and reports numerous cases of inhuman treatment, torture, and rape.

• Four English human rights militants armed with a hammer gain entry into the British Aerospace premises and damage a Hawk aircraft leaving for Indonesia. A similar aircraft had been used for bombing East Timor.

JAN 16 Negotiations between the Portuguese and the Indonesian foreign affairs ministers in London under the aegis of the United Nations.

JAN 24 The Indonesian Commission of Human Rights opens a representative office in Dili.

FEB During his visit to East Timor, Cardinal Roger Etchegaray, president of the Pontifical Council for Justice and Peace, makes it known that the Vatican does not wish to include East Timor in the Indonesian Episcopal conference. He also criticizes the Indonesian army's disrespect for human rights and reaffirms the necessity of solving the conflict while respecting the cultural and religious identity of the East Timorese.

FEB 29 The Portuguese prime minister António Gutteres meets President Suharto and asks for the release of Xanana Gusmão.

MAR 19/22 Second round of talks begun in June 1995 among the groups of the East Timorese diaspora at Burg Schlaining (Austria).

JUN The army opens fire on demonstrators at Baucau, causing the death of at least two persons. One hundred and sixty-five others are arrested.

OCT 11 The Nobel Peace Prize is jointly awarded to Carlos Filipe Ximenes Belo, bishop of Dili, and José Ramos Horta, the overseas representative of the East Timorese resistance. The prize would be given to them in Oslo on December 10.

1997

MAR 19 The East Timorese priest, Basílio do Nascinento, is appointed bishop of Baucau by the Vatican, in the name of the Italian diocese of Settimunicia.

MAR 27 The special envoy of the UN Jamsheed Marker meets Xanana Gusmão in prison.

APR 2 Opening of a new Catholic radio station, the first means of independent communication authorized by the Indonesian administration in twenty-one years of occupation.

APR 16 A resolution of the Human Rights Commission of the UN condemns the repeated Indonesian excesses and asks Jakarta to allow its special rapporteur on torture to visit East Timor once again.

1997 (*CONT.*)

MAY Manuel Carrascalão, a member since 1982 of the East Timorese provincial assembly set up by Indonesia, becomes a dissident.

JUN 27 Capture and execution of David Alex, the vice commandant of Falintil.

JUL 15 During his visit to Indonesia, Nelson Mandela, the South African president, openly demands a meeting with Xanana Gusmão. He declares that the release of the latter is indispensable for solving the Timorese problem.

AUG The Asian crisis hits Indonesia hard. The crash of the rupiah and the bankruptcy of some fifteen banks push two-thirds of the population below the poverty line.

OCT Manuel Carrascalão launches the movement for the Reconciliation and the Unity of the People of Timor (GRPRTT).

NOV 7 A report on the violence committed on the Timorese is submitted to the special UN rapporteur on violence against women.

1998

MAR General Suharto, in power since 1965, is reelected for a seventh presidential term.

APR 23–27 National Timorese convention in Lisbon. The CNRM becomes the CNRT (National Council of Timorese Resistance), whose president and vice president are Xanana Gusmão (in prison in Indonesia) and José Ramos Horta.

MAY A large number of Indonesian students take to the streets and occupy the parliament in Jakarta. They denounce collusion, corruption, and nepotism (termed, in short, as KKN) of the regime.

MAY 21 General Suharto is forced to resign. His vice president, Jusuf Habibie, replaces him.

MAY 26 Two Indonesian human rights militants, Muchtar Pakpahan and Sri Bintang Pamungkas, express their support to Xanana Gusmão on coming out of the Cipinang prison, where they were detained as political prisoners along with the East Timorese leader.

JUN 9 Three weeks after coming to power, President Habibie declares his intention of proposing a special status for East Timor.

JUN 15 Demonstration by 15,000 students in Dili demanding a referendum on self-determination and the release of Xanana Gusmão. Between June 15 and mid-July, 65,000 Indonesians leave the territory.

JUL 19 Bishop Belo of Dili meets Jamsheed Marker, the special representative of the UN secretary-general, at Baucau.

AUG 5 Fresh rounds of talks between Portugal and Indonesia.

1998 (*CONT.*)

AUG 12 Two Indonesian officers, Major General Damiri and Colonel Tono Suratman, ask the Timorese militia leaders they had trained (João Tavares, Eurico Guterres, and Cancio Carvalho) to organize themselves "for protecting integration."

AUG 21 Xanana Gusmão rejects the proposal for autonomy by the Indonesian government.

OCT 11 Thirty thousand persons organize a mar in Dili demanding the resignation of the pro-Indonesian governor Abílio Osório Soares.

NOV 2 Bishop Belo, bishop of Dili and Nobel Peace Prize winner, asks that Xanana Gusmão be included in the talks on the future of East Timor.

NOV 10 Arrival in East Timor of four hundred Kopassus commandos, who join the six thousand new soldiers sent from August to October.

NOV 20 The UN secretary-general expresses his concern about the mounting violence. The talks between Lisbon and Jakarta are suspended.

DEC 31 The Indonesian government frees sixty-two political prisoners, of whom twenty-six are Timorese, but continues to hold Xanana Gusmão prisoner.

1999

EARLY JAN Several cases of missing persons, tortures, and assassinations are reported by the organizations defending human rights. The former governor, Mário Carrascalão, declares that the Indonesian army distributed at least 12,000 arms to anti-separatist militia.

JAN 14 The European parliament condemns the repression of East Timorese civilians. It asks the Indonesian government to withdraw its troops and free the political prisoners.

JAN 27 The Indonesian president B. J. Habibie declares that he will ask the parliament (MPR) to grant independence to East Timor if it rejects the proposal of autonomy that he intends to offer.

JAN 28 Beginning of the negotiations between Jamsheed Marker, special UN representative on the East Timor question, and the delegates of the Portuguese and Indonesian foreign affairs ministries.

FEB 14 General Sudjarat, spokesman of the Indonesian armed forces, admits that the army supplies arms to the militia "for protecting the civilians from the Fretilin guerrillas."

FEB 18 The International Committee of the Red Cross asks the Indonesian government to disarm the militia.

1999 (*CONT.*)

FEB 22 General Wiranto, commander in chief of the Indonesian armed forces, declares that he will continue deploying the militia "to help the police maintain security."

MAR 11 The UN secretary-general announces that Portugal and Indonesia have arrived at an agreement in principle for organizing a "direct" consultation with the population of East Timor.

APR 5–6 Sixty-two dead and fourteen missing after the attack on the Liquiça church by the militia supported by the Indonesian army.

APR 17 Firing in the house of Manuel Carrascalão, one of the pro-separatist leaders who had requested army protection against the militia. At least eleven people die.
  • The UN secretary-general deplores the "apparent incapability of the Indonesian army to control violence and protect the population."

APR 21 Signature of an agreement between the militia and the resistance (Falintil) in order to form a joint commission of peace and stability.

APR 23 According to the Catholic church, at least forty persons were killed in the region of Suai.

APR 24 During a meeting with an Australian delegation, President Habibie admits his inability to disarm the militia.

APR 28 Bishop Basílio do Nascimento of Baucau declares that after the attack on his house, several militiamen tried to exonerate themselves by telling him they had been drugged by the army.

APR 30 Stanley Roth, American deputy secretary of state for the Asia-Pacific region, condemns the impunity enjoyed by the militia.

MAY 1 Megawati Sukarnoputri announces that she will cancel the proposed referendum if her party (PDI-Perjuangan) wins the Indonesian legislative polls.

MAY 5 Portugal, the UN, and Indonesia sign an agreement that defines the main modalities of the "popular consultation" slated for August 8, 1999.

MAY 18 More than thirty persons are killed by the militia in Atara.

MAY 28 The Justice and Peace Commission reports that the militia is in the process of drawing up a list of separatist leaders with the help of the Indonesian intelligence services.

JUN 1 Arrival in Dili of Ian Martin, the new representative of the UN secretary-general on the East Timor issue.

JUN 7 Indonesian legislative elections. Golkar, the party of former President Suharto and his successor B. J. Habibie, is defeated for the first time.

1999 (*CONT.*)

JUN 11 The Security Council establishes UNAMET (United Nations Assistance Mission in East Timor) to supervise the referendum.

• The Australian foreign affairs minister confirms having information proving that the Indonesian army actively encourages and supports the militia.

JUN 18 Ian Martin declares that tens of thousands of Timorese had to flee following the violence of the militia backed by Indonesia.

JUL 8 Mary Robinson, the UN human rights high commissioner, declares that she is worried about the attacks against UN personnel by armed militia.

JUL 10 Falintil proposes a new ceasefire.

JUL 14 General Wiranto, commander in chief of the Indonesian armed forces, refuses an interim force of the UN.

JUL 16 After several delays attributed to violence, enrollment on the electoral rolls for the referendum finally begins (until August 4). The total number of voters rises to 451,792, of whom 438,000 are in East Timor.

AUG 8 Signing of a code of good conduct between pro-separatists and anti-separatists.

AUG 19 Ian Martin, the representative of the UN secretary-general for East Timor, demands the withdrawal of the Indonesian officers actively involved with the militia.

AUG 20 The new outbreak of violence gives rise to fears that the referendum cannot take place before the end of UNAMET's term, fixed for the end of August.

AUG 26 The UN Security Council extends the term of UNAMET until November 30, 1999.

• Eurico Guterres, one of the pro-Indonesian militia leaders, declares to fifteen thousand of his supporters that East Timor will become a "sea of fire" if the separatists win.

AUG 28 Ali Alatas, the Indonesian foreign affairs minister, rejects the proposal of sending a peacekeeping force.

AUG 29 The militia destroys the offices of CNRT in Dili, Oecussi, and Los Palos.

AUG 30 The day of the referendum. More than 97 percent of East Timorese vote. Several acts of violence force the closing of seven polling booths momentarily in the district of Ermera.

AUG 31 The militia attacks the cities of Dili, Gleno, Aileu, Ermera, Ambeno, and Maliana. Three Timorese members of the UNAMET team are killed.

• Ali Alatas, the Indonesian foreign affairs minister, lauds the manner in which the referendum was conducted.

1999 (*CONT.*)

SEP 2 Special UN envoy Jamsheed Marker asks the Security Council to be prepared to send an international intervention force later on.

SEP 3 General Wiranto announces that in order to be prepared for "any possible circumstances," two new battalions (two thousand men) had been sent to East Timor.

SEP 4 Official announcement of the results of the referendum: 344,580 East Timorese (78.5 percent of the population) voted in favor of independence. Violence provoked by the militia and the Indonesian army oblige all the UN personnel to take shelter in Dili.

SEP 6 President Habibie declares martial law in East Timor. Numerous massacres are reported in the days that follow (at least two hundred persons in the Ave Maria Church in Suai, fifty in the police station in Maliana, twenty-five in the Camara Ecclesiastica in Dili, and an undetermined number in the residence of the bishop of Dili, which is completely destroyed). The Indonesian army organizes the displacement, often under pressure, of 300,000 East Timorese to West Timor and the neighboring islands.

SEP 7 Bishop Belo of Dili is evacuated to Darwin, Australia, while Xanana Gusmão is freed from his residence under surveillance; he seeks asylum in the UK embassy in Jakarta.

SEP 8 The Indonesian human rights commission condemns the incidents of violence and admits the involvement of the peacekeeping force of the archipelago.

• The Indonesian president Habibie reiterates his refusal to send an international peacekeeping force.

SEP 9 The UN secretary-general decides to repatriate his officers to Australia. Some of them refuse to leave the territory.

• During a meeting of the APEC in Auckland, the Western countries say that they are ready to envisage the sending of an international force of fifteen thousand men to East Timor.

SEP 10 American president Bill Clinton declares that the involvement of the Indonesian army with the militia is "not acceptable" and demands the suspension of military relations with Indonesia.

SEP 11 The UN secretary-general asks the Indonesian government to accept the sending of a multinational intervention force, failing which, Indonesia will find itself charged with crimes against humanity.

1999 (*CONT.*)
- Sir Henry Greenstock, British ambassador to the UN authorized to go to Dili, defines the situation prevailing in the territory as "hell on earth."

SEP 12 The UN Security Council firmly condemns the Indonesian action in East Timor. The declaration is not the result of a vote but all the members unite and take the initiative.
- The Indonesian government accepts the sending of a peacekeeping force.

SEP 13 The Indonesian government authorizes parachute drops of humanitarian aid for the hundreds of thousands of Timorese who had taken shelter in the mountains.

SEP 14 The European Union bans the sale of arms to Indonesia.

SEP 15 The UN Security Council approves the deployment of INTERFET (International Force for East Timor), an international intervention force placed under Australian command.

SEP 17 The Indonesian army begins its withdrawal from East Timor.

SEP 19 Major General Peter Cosgrove, commandant of INTERFET, arrives in Dili.

SEP 21 The withdrawal of the Indonesian battalion 745 causes severe destruction and the death of a Dutch journalist.

SEP 27 In the face of the great destruction and the number of victims, the UN High Commission for Refugees (UNHCR) demands the setting up of an international inquiry commission.

OCT 3 INTERFET strengthens the western frontier.

OCT 8 Beginning of the return of displaced people to East Timor.

OCT 13 A first count by the UN indicates that four hundred thousand East Timorese (45 percent of the population) is reported missing and must be in the mountains or in Indonesia.

OCT 18 The Indonesian assembly (MPR) officially recognizes the results of the referendum of August 30, 1999, and cancels the text of July 15, 1976, concerning the integration of East Timor.

OCT 19 The governor of the Indonesian province of Nusa Tenggara Timur (including West Timor) declares that 284,414 refugees are present in his territory.

OCT 20 The Indonesian parliament elects Abdurahman Wahid as president of the republic.

OCT 25 The Security Council sets up a provisional administration, UNTAET (United Nations Transitional Administration in East Timor), placed under the direction of Brazilian Sergio Vieira de Mello, who consults an East Timorese advisory National Council.

1999 (*CONT.*)

NOV 1 Departure of the last of the Indonesian troops from East Timor.

DEC 17 Sponsors for the reconstruction of East Timor meet in Tokyo and five hundred million dollars are released. The country now goes by the Tetum name Timor Lorosa'e (Timor sunrise) along with the Portuguese name Timor-Leste.

2000

JAN 12 Signing of a memorandum between UNTAET and the Indonesian army on the administration of the frontier between the two countries.

JAN 22 The American dollar is chosen as the temporary currency of the country without excluding the possibility of creating a national currency in the future.

JAN 31 The Indonesian Commission on the Violation of Human Rights in East Timor, formed in 1999, submits its report. It lists in detail the extortions, lays emphasis on the responsibility of the Indonesian army, and indicates that General Wiranto, commander in chief of the armed forces, could be considered as one of the main culprits. The commission declares that the facts reveal crimes against humanity and demands the constitution of an international tribunal.

FEB 5 The pro-Indonesian militia regroups under the name UNTAS (Uni Aswain Timor, "Union of the heroes of Timor," unrelated to the UN).

FEB 12 Visit of the Portuguese president Jorge Sampaio to East Timor.

FEB 29 Visit of the Indonesian president Abdurahman Wahid to East Timor. He apologizes to the East Timorese people for "all that happened in the past."

APR 11 Signing of a protocol of agreement between the Indonesian army and the UNTAET military wing concerning the control of the frontier between East Timor and Indonesia.

APR 29 Opening of a postal service in East Timor.

JUL 24 Death of the first soldier of the intervention force during a confrontation with the militia on the western frontier.

SEP 6 In West Timor, the attack on the office of the High Commission for Refugees by the pro-Indonesian militia leads to the death of three UN personnel.

SEP 7 AND 8 Faced with the inability of Indonesia to guarantee their safety, 462 foreigners working for international and non-government organizations leave West Timor.

DEC 11 First indictments for crimes against humanity by the Dili Court of Justice under the aegis of the UN for acts committed in 1999 by the militia and the Indonesian army.

2000 (*CONT.*)

DEC 31 The American immigration services refuse to give a visa to ex-General Prabowo Subianto, son-in-law of ex-president Suharto, due to the charges of torture leveled against him.

2001

JAN 25 First conviction of a militiaman by the Dili Court of Justice João Fernandes, of the militia Dadurus Merah Putih, sentenced to twelve years in prison for murdering a village chief.

FEB 1 Dissolution of Falintil and founding of FDTL (Force for the Defense of Timor-Leste).

MAR 16 Decree of UNTAET for the election of a constituent assembly and beginning of registration of voters (until June 23).

MAR 19 Xanana Gusmão dissolves the common platform of the CNRT in order to allow free competition among the parties.

MAR 27 The district court of Washington (USA) begins the trial in absentia of General Johny Lumintang for his participation in planning and supervising acts of violence committed by the anti-separatist militia in 1999 while he was the chief of the Indonesian army.

MAR 29 Xanana Gusmão resigns from the National Advisory Council established by the UNTAET after a disagreement over the modalities of consulting the population for drawing up the constitution.

APR 9 Manuel Carrascalão is elected as the head of the National Council.

APR 23 The Indonesian government establishes an ad hoc court of justice in Jakarta (KEPPRESS 53/2001) for the trial of crimes committed after the referendum of August 30, 1999.

MAY 1 Eurico Guterres, one of the principal pro-Indonesian militia leaders, is sentenced to six months' imprisonment by the ad hoc Indonesian tribunal for the crimes committed in East Timor. He is freed after three weeks in detention.

JUN 6–7 While 185,000 displaced people returned to East Timor and the Indonesian authorities identified only 108,359 "refugees" a few weeks earlier, a poll organized in West Timor shows that 98.9 percent of the 292,491 refugees might have chosen to remain in Indonesia.

JUL 6 Renegotiations with Australia over the agreement on petroleum resources in the Timor Sea. East Timor obtains 90 percent of the royalties of the central zone, which is the most promising.

JUL 8 National Unity Pact among all political factions in East Timor for the election of the constituent assembly.

2001 (*CONT.*)

JUL 10 More than a month after the consultation organized by Indonesia in the displaced East Timorese community in West Timor, the officer in charge of the UN High Commission for Refugees fears that only a very small part of the number of families wanting to return were repatriated.

JUL 13 UNTAET establishes a Commission for Reception, Truth, and Reconciliation (CRTR, decision 2001/10), whose purpose is to throw light on the events that took place between April 1974 and October 1999.

JUL 14 An expert UN mission visiting West Timor concludes that the militia "continues to be a veritable threat to the United Nations operations" and that UNTAS "shows a tendency to manipulate many refugees and is interested in preventing them from returning home."

• With the approach of the elections, UNTAET dissolves the advisory National Council.

JUL 23 Abdurahman Wahid is forced to step down from the post of the president of the republic in favor of his vice president Megawati Sukarnoputri, daughter of the first president of the republic.

• East Timor is granted permission to be an observer at the ASEAN inter-ministerial conference held in Hanoi.

JUL 27 The bishop of Atambua (West Timor) complains of extortion by militiamen of East Timorese origin "who destroy dwellings and shops."

AUG 17 Eurico Guterres, one of the principal leaders of the pro-Indonesian militia whom the Indonesian justice exempted from serving his sentence, is invited by the new president to attend the national ceremonies on August 17 in Jakarta.

AUG 30 Elections for the constituent assembly in East Timor, with the participation of 94 percent of enrolled voters. Fretilin wins 57.4 percent of the vote.

AUG 31 João Tavares and Domingos Soares, the two principal pro-Indonesian militia leaders (UNTAS) domiciled in Indonesia, reject the election results in East Timor and reiterate their desire to "continue to fight against independence till the end."

SEP The European Union and the United States contribute six million euros and three million dollars respectively for the resettlement of "refugees" in West Timor.

SEP 12 First meeting between the new Indonesian president Megawati Sukarnoputri and the representatives of East Timor Sergio Vieira de Mello (chief of UNTAET), Xanana Gusmão, Mari Alkatiri (prime minister), and José Ramos Horta (minister for foreign affairs).

2001 (*CONT.*)

OCT 22 The announcement by the Japanese government that it has sent a battalion of six hundred engineers from its self-defense force arouses intense agitation in East Timor.

DEC 30 On taking oath, Megawati Sukarnoputri, the new Indonesian president, declares that the army should try hard to guard the unity of the country and that as long as it stays within the framework of the law, it must do its duty without asking itself questions on human rights.

2002

JAN 14 Arrival in Dili of Leandro Despouy, the president of the UN Human Rights Commission.

JAN 15 Indonesian president Megawati Sukarnoputri appoints an ad hoc court of justice for the crimes in East Timor. Its jurisdiction is limited to the extortions committed between April and September 1999 in three of the thirteen districts of the territory.

JAN 16 The bishop of Dili, Carlos Ximenes Belo, warns the population of the risk of yielding to the mentality of living on aid due to the easy money available from UN subsidies.

FEB 26 First trilateral meeting of the representatives of the governments of East Timor, Indonesia, and Australia.

FEB 28 The authorities of East Timor and Indonesia sign an agreement on the demarcation of their common frontier.

MAR 22 Adoption of a national constitution.

APR 4 Kamalesh Sharma, an Indian national, is appointed to head the UN representation in East Timor from May 21, 2002.

MAY 20 Independence of Timor-Leste.

Photo Stéphane Dovert

Timorese in the mountains

Xanana Gusmão reviewing Falintil troops around 1983

Photo Frédéric Durand

New Zealand soldiers at the Indonesian/East Timor border, 2001

Modern East-Timorese coin depicting a traditional boat

Bibliography

General

Barbedo de Magalhães, António Pinto, ed. *Timor-Leste : Interesses internacionais e actor locais*. Porto: Afrontamento, 2007.

Castro, Affonso de. *As Possessões Portuguezas na Oceania*. Lisboa: Imprensa Nacional, 1867.

Cinatti, Ruy. *Arquitectura Timorense*. Lisbon: Instituto de Investigação Científica Tropical, Museu de Etnologia, 1987.

———. *Motivos artísticos Timorenses e a sua Intergração*. Lisbon: Instituto de Investigação Científica Tropical, Museu de Etnologia, 1987.

Defert, Gabriel. *Timor-Est, le génocide oublié*. Paris: L'Harmattan, 1992.

Dunn, James. *Timor: A People Betrayed*. Milton, Queensland: Jacaranda Press, 1983.

Durand, Frédéric. *Catholicisme et protestantisme dans l'île de Timor 1556–2003, construction d'une identité chrétienne et engagement politique contemporain*. Bangkok: IRASEC (Institut de Recherche sur l'Asie du Sud-Est Contemporaine): 2004.

———. *East Timor: A Country at the Crossroads of Asia and the Pacific*. Chiang Mai: Silkworm Books, 2006.

———. *Timor 1250–2005, 750 ans de cartographie et de voyages*. Bangkok: IRASEC 2006.

Felgas, Helio A. Esteves. *Timor Português*. Lisbon: Agência geral do Ultramar, 1956.

GERTiL (Grupo de Estudos de Reconstrução de Timor Leste). *Atlas de Timor Leste*. Lisbon: Faculdade de Arquitectura da Universidade Técnica de Lisboa, 2002.

Grupo de Trabalho do Ministério da Educação, ed. Coord. by Rui Manuel Louriero. *Onde Nasce o Sândalo, Os Portugueses em Timor nos Séculos XVI e XVII*. Algueirão: Grupo de Trabalho do Ministério da Educação, 1995.

Gunn, Geoffrey C. *Timor Loro Sae: 500 Years*. Macau: Livros do Oriente, 1999.

Gusmão, Xanana. *Timor Leste, um Povo, uma Pátria*. Lisbon: Edições Colibri, 1994.

Loureiro, João. *Postais Antiguos & Outro Memórias de Timor.* Macau: Fundação, 1999.

Louriero, Rui Manuel. *See* Grupo de Trabalho do Ministério da Educação.

Metzner, Joachim K. *Man and Environment in Eastern Timor: A Geoecological Analysis of the Baucau-Viqueque Area as a Possible Basis for Regional Planning.* Canberra: Australian National University, 1977.

Oliveira, Luna de. *Timor na História de Portugal.* 4 vols. Facsimile of the 1949 edition. Lisbon: Fundação Oriente, 2004.

Ormeling, Ferdinand Jan. *The Timor Problem, A Geographical Interpretation of an Underdeveloped Island.* The Hague: Martinus Nijhoff, 1956.

Ramos Horta, José. *Funu, the Unfinished Saga of East-Timor.* Trenton, NJ: Red Sea Press, 1987.

Bibliographical Works

Belo, Carlos Filipe Ximenes. *Subsídio para a bibliografia de Timor Loro-Sa'e. Uma listagem cronológica de livros, ensaios, documentos e artigos desde 1515 a 2000.* Lisbon: CEPCEP, 2002.

Berlie, Jean. *East Timor: A Bibliography.* Paris: Les Indes Savantes, 2001.

Pélissier, René. *Du Sahara à Timor 700 livres analysés (1980–1990) sur l'Afrique et l'Insulinde ex-ibériques.* Orgeval: Pélissier éditeur, 1991.

Roff, Sue Rabbitt. *East Timor: A Bibliography, 1970–1993.* Canberra: Peace Research Centre, Research School of Pacific and Asian Studies, Australian National University, 1994.

Rowland, Ian. *Timor, including the Islands of Roti and Ndao.* Oxford: Clio, 1992.

Sherlock, Kevin. *A Bibliography of Timor.* Canberra: Research School of Pacific Studies, Research Series NA/4, Australian National University, 1980.

Main Sources by Chapter

Chapter 1 Prehistoric Timor

Almeida, António de. "Da Pré-História de Timor Portugues." In *Memórias da Academia das Ciências de Lisboa,* 27–47. Tomo 19. Lisbon: Academy of Sciences, 1976.

Cinatti, Ruy. "As pinturas rupestres de Timor." *Colóquio* 23 (1963): 49–59.

Glover, Ian. *Archaeology in East-Timor 1966–67.* Canberra: Research School of Pacific and Asian Studies, Australian National University, 1986.

Hull, Geoffrey. "The Basic Lexical Affinities of Timor's Austronesian Languages: A Preliminary Investigation." *Studies in Languages and Culture of East Timor* 1 (1998): 97–174.

———. "The Papuan Languages of Timor." *Studies in Languages and Culture of East Timor* 6 (2004): 23–99.

Lape, Peter V. "Chronology of Fortified Settlements in East Timor." *Journal of Islands and Coastal Archeology* 1 (2006): 285–97.

———. "Fortification as a Human Response to Late Holocène Climate Change in East Timor." *Archeol. Oceania* 43 (2008): 11–21.

Lape, Peter V., Sue O'Connor, and Nick Burningham. "Rock Art: A Potential Source of Information about Past Maritime Technology in South-East Asia-Pacific Region." *International Journal of Nautical Archeology* 36, no. 2 (2007): 238–53.

O'Connor, Sue. "Nine New Painted Rock Art Sites from East Timor in the Context of the Western Pacific Region." *Journal of Archeology for Asia and the Pacific* 42 (2003): 96–128.

O'Connor, Sue, and Peter Veth. "Early Holocene Shell Fish Hooks from Lene Hara Cave, East Timor Establish Complex Fishing Technology Was in Use in Island South East Asia Five Thousand Years before Austronesian Settlement." *Antiquity* 79, no. 304 (2005): 249–56.

O'Connor, Sue, and Ken Aplin. "A Matter of Balance: An Overview of Pleistocene Occupation History and the Impact of the Last Glacial Phase in East Timor and the Aru Islands, Eastern Indonesia." *Archaeology in Oceania* 42, no. 3 (2007): 82–90.

O'Connor, Sue, Matthew Spriggs, and Peter Veth. "Direct Dating of Shell Beads from Lene Hara Cave, East Timor." *Australian Archaelogy* 55 (2002): 18–21.

Oliveira, Nuno Vasco. "Subsistence Archeobotany: Food Production and the Agricultural Transition in East Timor." PhD diss., Department of Archaeology and Natural History, Australian National University, Canberra, 2008.

Spriggs, Matthew, Sue O'Connor, and Peter Veth. "Vestige of Early Pre-agricultural Economy in the Landscape of East-Timor." In *Fishbones and Glittering Emblems*, edited by Anna Karlström and Anna Källén, 49–58. Stockholm: Museum of Far Eastern Antiquities, 2003.

Chapter 2 Major External Contacts before the Portuguese

Eccles, Lance. "Early Chinese Accounts of Timor." *Studies in Languages and Culture of East Timor* 6 (2004): 178–87.

Hirth, Freidrich, and W. W. Rockhill, trans. *Chau Ju-Kua: His Work on the Chinese and Arab Trade in the Twelfth and Thirteenth Centuries, entitled Chu-Fan-Chï.* Taipei: Ch'eng-Wen Publishing Company, 1970.

Mills, J.V. "Chinese Navigators in Insulinde about A.D. 1500." *Archipel* 18 (1979): 69–93.

Ptak, Roderich. "Some references to Timor in Old Chinese Records." *Ming Studies* 17 (1983): 37–48.

Tibbetts, G. R. *A Study of the Arabic Texts Containing Material on South-East Asia.* Leiden: E. J. Brill, 1979.

Chapter 3 Traditional Societies

Berthe, Louis. *Bei Gua, itinéraire des ancêtres, mythes bunaq de Timor.* Paris: Editions du CNRS, 1972.

Cinatti, Ruy. *Arquitectura Timorense.* Lisbon: Instituto de Investigação Cientifica Tropical, Museu de Etnologica, 1987.

Duarte, Jorge Barros. *Timor, ritos e mitos Ataúros.* Lisbon: Instituto de Cultura e Língua Portuguesa, 1984.

Fox, James J. *Harvest of the Palm: Ecological Change in Eastern Indonesia.* Cambridge: Harvard University Press, 1977.

Friedberg, Claudine. "Agricultures timoraises." *Etudes Rurales* 53–56 (1974): 375–405.

Hicks, David. *Tetum Ghosts and Kin.* CA: Mayfield Publishing Company, 1976.

King, Margaret. *Eden to Paradise.* London: Hodder and Soughton, 1963.

McWilliam, Andrew. "Prospects for the Sacred Grove: Valuing *Lulic* Forests on Timor." *The Asia Pacific Journal of Anthropology* 2, no. 2 (2001): 89–113.

Renard Clamagirand, Brigitte. *Marobo, une société ema de Timor.* Paris: SELAF, 1982.

Schulte-Nordholt, Herman Gerrit. *The Political System of the Atoni of Timor.* The Hague: Martinus Nijhoff, 1971.

Therik, Tom. *Wehale, the Female Land: Traditions of a Timorese Ritual Centre.* Canberra: Pandanus Books, 2004.

Thomaz, Luis Filipe. *Notas sobre a vida marítima em Timor.* Lisbon: Centro de Estudos de Marinha, 1977.

Traube, Elizabeth G. *Cosmology and Social Life: Ritual Exchange among the Mambai of East Timor.* Chicago: University of Chicago Press, 1986.

Chapter 4 The Beginning of Western Influence, 1512–1642

Boxer, C. R. *Francisco Vieira de Figueiredo, A Portuguese Merchant-Adventurer in South East Asia, 1624–1667.* The Hague: Martinus Nijhoff, 1967.

———. *The Topasses of Timor.* Amsterdam: Koninklijke Vereeniging Indisch Instituut (Mededeling no. LXXIII Afdeling Volkenkunde no. 24): 1947.

Grupo de Trabalho do Ministério da Educação, ed. (Louriero, Rui Manuel, coord.) *Onde Nasce o Sândalo, Os Portugueses em Timor nos Séculos XVI e XVII.* Algueirão: Grupo de Trabalho do Ministério da Educação, 1995.

Hägerdal, Hans. "Servião and Belu: Colonial Conceptions and the Geographical Partition of Timor." *Studies on Asia,* series 3, vol. 3, no. 1 (2006): 49–64. Online. http://studiesonasia.illinoisstate.edu

Leitão, Comandante Humberto. *Os Portugueses em Solor e Timor de 1515 a 1702.* Lisbon: Tip. da Liga dos Combatentes da Grande Guerra, 1948.

Morais, Ten.-Coronel A. Faria de. *Sólor e Timor.* Lisbon: Agência geral das Colónias, 1943.

Pires, Tomé. *The Suma Oriental and The Book of Francisco Rodrigues.* 2 vols. New Delhi: Asian Educational Services, 1990.

Chapter 5 The Rise of the Portuguese and Topasses, 1641–1769

Boxer, C. R. *The Topasses of Timor.* Mededeling no. 73, Afdeling Volkenkunde no. 24. Amsterdam: Koninklijke Vereeniging Indisch Instituut, 1947.

Dampier, William. *A Voyage to New Holland, the English Voyage of Discovery to the South Seas in 1699.* Gloucester: Allan Soutton, 1981.

Hägerdal, Hans. "Rebellions or Factionalism? Timorese Forms of Resistance in an Early Colonial Context, 1650–1769." *KITLV (Bijdragen tot de Taal-, Land- en Volkenkunde)* 163, no. 2 (2007): 1–33.

———. *Lords of the Land, Lords of the Sea: Conflict and Adaptation in Early Colonial Timor, 1600–1800.* Leiden: KITLV, 2012.

Sá, Artur Basílio de. *A Planta de Cailaco 1727.* Lisbon: Agência geral das Colónias, 1949.

Chapter 6 Alliances and Confrontations in Eastern Timor, 1769–1852

Almeida, António de. *O Oriente de Expressão Portuguesa.* Lisbon: Fundação Oriente, 1994.

Belo, Carlos Filipe Ximenes. *Os Antigos reinos de Timor-Leste.* Baucau: Edição Tipografia Diocesana, 2011.

Dores, Raphael das. *Apontamentos para um Diccionario Chorographico de Timor.* Lisbon: Imprensa Nacional, 1903.

Labrousse, Pierre. "Images de Timor en France (1812–1824)." *Archipel* 62 (2001): 71–90.

Lombard-Jourdan, Anne. "Un mémoire inédit de F.E. de Rosily sur l'île de Timor (1772)." *Archipel* 23 (1982): 83–104.

Chapter 7 Colonial Wars of the Second Half of the Nineteenth Century

Ferreira, João Gomes. "Calculo approximativo da população da parte portugueza de Timor, feito em 1882." *Boletim da Sociedade de Geographia de Lisboa* 20a, no. 10 (1902): 129–31.

Oliveira Pinto da França Tamagnini, Maria Isabel. *Diário de uma viagem a Timor (1882–1883)*. Porto: Centro Português de Estudos do Sudeste Asiático, 2002.

Roque, Ricardo. *Headhunting and Colonialism: Anthropology and the Circulation of Human Skulls in the Portuguese Empire, 1870–1930*. Cambridge Imperial and Post-Colonial Studies. London: Palgrave Macmillan, 2010.

Wallace, Alfred Russel. *The Malay Archipelago*. Singapore: Graham Brash, 1869/1989.

Chapter 8 The Manufahi Wars, 1895–1912

Oliveira, Luna de. *Timor na História de Portugal*. 4 vols. Facsimile of the 1949 edition. Lisbon: Fundação Oriente, 2004.

Pélissier, René. *Les campagnes coloniales du Portugal 1844–1941*. Paris: Pygmalion, 2004.

———. *Timor en guerre, le crocodile et les Portugais (1847–1913)*. Orgeval: Pélissier éditeur, 1996.

Chapter 9 Political and Economic Transformations and Final Border Demarcation

Castro, Affonso de. *As Possessões Portuguezas na Oceania*. Lisbon: Imprenso Nacional, 1867.

Clarence-Smith, Gervaise. *The Third Portuguese Empire 1825–1975: A Study in Economic Imperialism*. Manchester: Manchester University Press, 1985.

Heyman, Albertus. *De Timor-Tractaten (1859 en 1893)*. Leiden: S. C. van Doesburgh, 1895.

Lains e Silva, Hélder. *Timor e a cultura do café*. Porto: Imprensa Portuguesa, 1956.

Chapter 10 World War II and the Japanese Occupation, 1941–1945

Borda d'Água, Flávio. *Le Timor Oriental face à la Seconde Guerre mondiale (1941–1945)*. Lisbon: Instituto diplomático, 2007.

Bretes, Maria da Graça. *Timor entre invadores 1941–1945.* Lisbon: Livros Horizonte, 1989.

Callinan, Bernard. *Independent Company: The 2/2 and 2/4 Australian Independent Companies in East-Timor, 1941–1943.* Melbourne: William Heinemann, 1953.

Turner, Michele. *Telling East Timor: Personal Testimonies 1942–92.* Kensington: New South Wales University Press, 1992.

Chapter 11 The "Submissive" Alliance between Timorese and Portuguese, 1945–1974

Agência geral do Ultramar. *Relação da Primeira Viagem do Ministro do Ultramar as Províncias do Oriente, no Ano de MCMLII.* Vol. 2. Lisbon: Divisão de Publicações e Biblioteca, 1954.

Brito da Fonseca, Rui. *Monumentos Portugueses em Timor-Leste.* Porto: Orgal Impressores, 2005.

Instituto Superior de Ciências Socias e Politica Ultramarina, ed. *As Províncias do Oriente.* 2 vols. Lisbon: Instituto Superior de Ciências Socias e Politica Ultramarina, 1967.

Loureiro, João. *Postais antigos & outras memorias de Timor.* Lisbon: Fundação Macau, 1999.

Teixeira, Manuel. *Macau e a sua Diocese. X Missões de Timor.* Macau: Tipografia da Missão do Padraodo, 1974.

Themudo Barata, Filipe. *Timor Contemporâneo, da primeira ameaça da Indonesia ao nascer de uma nação.* Lisbon: Equilíbrio Editorial, 1998.

Vondra, J. Gert. *Timor Journey.* Pacific Journeys 3. Melbourne: Lansdowne, 1968.

Chapter 12 Political Awakening and Failure of the Decolonization Process, 1974–1975

Carrascalão, Mario Viegas. *Timor, Antes do Futuro.* Dili: Livraria Mau Huran, 2006.

Hill, Helen Mary. "Fretilin: The Origins, Ideologies and Strategies of a Nationalist Movement in East Timor." MA thesis. Monash University, 1978.

Jolliffe, Jill. *East Timor, Nationalism and Colonialism.* Queensland: University of Queensland Press, 1978.

Lemos Pires, Mário. *Decolonização de Timor, Missão Impossivel?* 3rd ed. Lisbon: Publicações Dom quixote, 1994.

Nicol, Bill. *Timor, the Stillborn Nation.* Melbourne: Visa Book, 1978.

Chapter 13 The Years of Armed Struggle, 1975–1989

Aditjondro, George J. *In the Shadow of Mount Ramelau: The Impact of the Occupation of East Timor.* Amsterdam: Indoc, 1994.

Budiardjo, Carmel, and Liem Soei Liong. *The War Against East Timor.* London: Zed Books, 1984.

Caldeira, Alfredo, coord. *Resistencia Timorense, Arquivo and Museu.* Dili: Instituto Camões, 2005.

Conway, Jude, ed. *Step by Step: Women of East Timor, Stories of Resistance and Survival.* Darwin: Charles Darwin University Press, 2010.

Lennox, Rowena. *Fighting Spirit of East Timor: The Life of Martinho da Costa Lopes.* Australia: Pluto Press, 2000.

Mattoso, José. *A dignidade, Konis Santana e a Resistência Timorense.* Lisbon: Temas e Debates, 2005.

Niner, Sarah, ed. *To Resist Is to win! The Autobiography of Xanana Gusmao.* Victoria, Australia: Aurora Books, 2000.

Retbøll, Torben, ed. *East Timor, Indonesia and the Western Democraties: A Collection of Documents.* Copenhagen: IWGIA documents, 1980.

Taylor, John G. *Indonesia's Forgotten War, The Hidden History of East Timor.* London: Zed Books, 1991.

Chapter 14 From Popular Demonstrations to Referendum, 1989–1999

Belo, Carlos Filipe Ximenes. *The Road to Freedom: A Collection of Speeches, Pastoral Letters, and Articles from 1997–2001.* Sydney: Caritas Australia, 2001.

Carey, Peter, and G. Carter Bentley. *East Timor at the Crossroads: The Forging of a Nation.* New York: Social Science Council, 1995.

Dunn, James. *Crimes against Humanity in East Timor, January to October 1999: Their Nature and Causes.* Report to UNTAET, Dili, 2001.

Inbaraj, Sonny. *East Timor, Blood and Tears in ASEAN.* Chiang Mai: Silkworm Books, 1997.

Kingsbury, Damien, ed. *Guns and Ballot Boxes: East Timor's Vote for Independence.* Clayton, Australia: Monash Asia Institute, 2000.

Kohen, Arnold S. *From the Place of the Dead: Bishop Belo and the Struggle for East Timor.* Oxford: Lion Publishing, 1999.

Mubyarto and Loekman Soetrisno, eds. *East Timor, the Impact of Integration: An Indonesian Socio-anthropological Study.* Australia: IRIP, 1990.

Pinto, Constâncio, and Matthew Jardine. *East Timor's Unfinished Struggle: Inside the Timorese Resistance. A Testimony*. Boston: South Ends Press, 1997.

Chapter 15 From Referendum to Independence, 1999–2002

Alkatiri, Mari. *Timor-Leste, O Caminho do Desenvolvimento, os primeiros anos de governação*. Lisbon: Lidel, 2006.

Babo Soares, Dionisio, Michael Maley, James J. Fox, and Anthony J. Regan. *Elections and Constitution Making in East Timor*. Canberra: Pandanus Books–Australian National University, 2003.

Bappeda Tingkat I dan Kanwil BPB Timor Timur. *Peta realisasi transmigrasi umum*. n.p.: Bappeda, 1995/96 and 1997.

Durand, Frédéric. *Timor-Leste en quête de repères, perspectives économico-politiques et intégration régionale 1999–2050*. Bangkok: IRASEC, 2008.

Fox, James, and Dionisio Babo Soares, eds. *Out of the Ashes: Destruction and Reconstruction of East Timor*. Adelaide: Crawford House, 2000.

Guedes, Armando Marques, and Nuno Canas Mendes, eds. *Ensaios sobre nacionalismos em Timor-Leste*. Lisbon: Colecção Biblioteca Diplomática do Ministério dos Negócios Estrangeiros, 2005.

Gunn, Geoffrey C., and Reyko Huang. *New Nation: United Nations Peace-Building in East Timor*. Macau: Tipografia Macau Hung Heng, 2006.

Gusmão, Xanana. *A Construção da Nação Timorense, desafios e oportunidades*. Lisbon: Lidel, 2004.

Hill, Hal, and João M. Saldanha, eds. *East Timor: Development Challenges of the World's Newest Nation*. Singapore: ISEAS-Asia Pacific Press, 2001.

KPP-HAM-TimTim. "Ringkasan Eksekutif Laporan Penyelidikan Pelanggaran Hak Asasi Manusia di Timor Timur." Jakarta, January 31, 2000.

Martin, Ian. *Self-Determination in East Timor: The United Nations, the Ballot, and International Intervention*. International Peace Academy Occasional Paper Series. Boulder: Lynne Rienner, 2001.

Thomaz, Luís Filipe. *Babel Loro Sa'e, O Problema linguístico de Timor-Leste*. Lisbon: Instituto Camões, 2002.

UNTAET and the World Bank. "Background Paper for the Interim Donors' Meeting on East Timor, " Dili, March 29, 2001.

Additional Sources of Maps and Illustrations

Note: See below for sources not already listed in the bibliography.

Agência geral das Colónias. *Timor, catalogue de l'exposition internationale d'Anvers*. Brussels and Lisbonne: August Puvrez, 1930.

Atlas van Tropisch Nederland. Gemilang, The Netherlands: Antiquarianbooksellers, 1938.

Carta da Província de Timor (Esboço). Ministério das Colónias, Comissão de Cartografia, 1927. 1:1,000,000.

Catálogo da Exposição de Pintura de Fausto Sampaio na Sociedade de Belas Artes. Lisbon, 1939.

Cinatti, Ruy Vaz Monteiro Gomes. *Estudos, ensaios e documentos V Reconhecimento das formações florestais no Timor Português*. Lisbon: Ministério das Colónias, 1950.

Colijn, H., ed. *Neerlands Indië, land en volk, geschiedenis en bestuur, bedrijf en samenleving*. 2 vols. Amsterdam: Elsevier, 1911-1912.

Corrêa, A. A. Mendes, António de Almeida, and Camarate França. "Sobre alguns exemplares com fácies paleolítica de Timor Português." *Memórias da Junta de Investigaçöes do Ultramar 2*, no. 50 (1964): 15-33.

Gent, L. F. van, et al. *Gedenkboek van Nederlandsch-Indië 1898-1923*. Batavia: G. Golff, 1923.

Hattori, Shino, and Stephen A. Wurm. *Language Atlas, Pacific Area*. Canberra: The Australian Academy of the Humanities in collaboration with the Japan Academy, 1981.

Martinho, J. S. *Timor, Quarto soculos de colonização portuguesa*. Porto: Livraria Progredior, 1943.

Matos, Artur Teodoro de. *Timor Português 1515-1769. Contribuição para a sua história*. Lisbon: University of Lisbon, Faculty of Letters, 1974.

Monk, Kathryn A., et al. *The Ecology of Nusa Tenggara and Maluku*. Singapore: Periplus Editions, 1997.

Oliveira, Barradas de. *Roteiro do Oriente*. Lisbon: Agência Geral do Ultramar, 1954.

Wallace, Alfred Russel. "L'archipel malaisien, patrie de l'orang-outang et de l'oiseau de paradis. Récits de l'homme et de la nature." *Journal autour du Monde*, 5 vols. Paris: Hachette, 1872.